THE GLOBALIZATION OF POLITICS

The Globalization of Politics

The Changed Focus of Political Action in the Modern World

Evan Luard

NEW YORK UNIVERSITY PRESS
Washington Square, New York

First published in the U.S.A. in 1990 by
NEW YORK UNIVERSITY PRESS
Washington Square
New York, NY 10003

Library of Congress Cataloging-in-Publication Data
Luard, Evan, 1926–
The globalization of politics: the changed focus of political action in the modern world / Evan Luard.
p. cm.
ISBN 0–8147–5047–8
1. International relations. 2. World politics—1945– 3. International economic relations. I. Title.
JX1391.L83 1990
327.1′1—dc20 89–14035
CIP

Printed in Great Britain

Contents

Introduction

For the contemporary citizen politics remains, as it has always been, essentially a national preoccupation: a struggle for power and influence undertaken within the arena of the national state.

The chief political actors are national political leaders and national political parties. Their political goal is power within the nation. The dominant political issues are those which arise within the national state: what should be the distribution of wealth and welfare in the national territory; what action to influence this should be taken by the national government; what policies to promote the national well-being should be advocated by national political parties; which such party will win the next (national) election? It is power, policies and politicians at the national level which are everywhere understood. It is true that there is occasional mention of "international politics". But this is generally seen as a synonym for "international relations", the relations undertaken between separate national states pursuing separate national interests: a diplomatic dialogue between diverse power-centres. It is those power-centres which remain the essential political entities. And it is therefore the struggle for power *within* each state which is still seen as the real stuff of politics.

It is the contention of the pages that follow that this represents an old-fashioned and misguided viewpoint. It derives from a time when what was of overwhelming importance to the citizen was the way power was exercised at state level. It was the actions taken by national governments which, traditionally, were decisive in determining their welfare. And it was therefore the contest for control of those governments, and the controversies which arose concerning the actions they took, which lay at the heart of political discussion. "Politics" was essentially national politics.

Today, with the breathtaking shrinkage of the world which has taken place over the last fifty years or so, those assumptions have been destroyed. The welfare of ordinary men and women no longer depends primarily on the actions of their own governments. It depends, far more, on actions and decisions reached, far beyond the frontiers of their own state, by other governments, or by international bodies taking decisions collectively. Political activity devoted to determining which political leader or which political party rules in their own state therefore becomes increasingly irrelevant. Only political activity which affects the decisions that are taken in the wider world without can now bring about the changes which matter most to them.

Some of the most important decisions, as within states, relate to economic affairs. The emergence of a single, closely interrelated international economy means that it is no longer the way their own local economy is managed by their own government which determines people's economic future. Whether they suffer from depression or inflation, whether unemployment is low or interest rates high, will depend not on the actions of their own or any single national government, but on actions that are taken by a large number of other governments around the world, or the decisions of international bodies such as the IMF: on exchange rates, reflation, monetary policy, the level of credit and other matters. Whether the price of oil, coffee or milk goes up or down will be determined not by their own or any single government, but by groups of governments elsewhere reaching decisions together: in OPEC, in the International Coffee Agreement, or within the EEC. It is the future of the international economy and not of any single national economy that matters. And it is the decisions that influence this that are important to individuals in every state.

This dependence on external decisions and events is only marginally affected by the geographical situation of each citizen. The great majority of the world's population who live in poorer and smaller countries are the most self-evidently dependent on actions taken in other states. Whether there will be a market for the exports they manufacture, what kind of price will be got for them, the terms on which their debts will be repaid, whether their nations can secure inward investment, or managerial skills, or the transfer of technology, all of these depend primarily on decisions reached elsewhere. But the inhabitants of medium-sized states too are deeply affected by external events – whether the US economy booms or declines, whether Japan and West Germany reflate or deflate, whether the stock markets in Hong Kong and London go up or down – and so by the economic policies pursued by other administrations. Even the inhabitants of the most powerful state on earth, the US, are dependent on decisions taken in other countries: decisions on the price of oil, reached by the governments of oil-producing countries; decisions on the purchase of dollars and dollar securities, reached by Japanese finance houses; decisions on interest rates and exchange rates reached by finance ministers in Western Europe. To individuals everywhere, therefore, decisions abroad now become more important than decisions at home. The important political developments are not national but global.

But it is not only in the economic field that the power over events has slipped beyond the control of any national state. In the field of security, equally, the significant decisions are reached beyond the boundaries of single nations. Only a few decades ago each nation provided individually for its own defence. Britain prided herself on her "splendid isolation". The US shunned "entangling alliances". Today no state can, by its own decisions alone, safeguard the lives of its citizens. Developments in military technology, the manufacture of weapons of vast destructive power, and the capacity to deliver them half way round the world at almost a moment's notice, mean that no country can any longer, unaided, defend itself and its population. Even the most powerful of all, the US and the Soviet Union, require to maintain alliances of like-minded nations, and to control protective belts around their borders – the glacis of Eastern Europe and Central America – to hold the enemy at a distance. Each feels obliged to intervene in other countries far beyond their own borders (for example, the US in Vietnam, the Soviet Union in Cuba), when they believe this essential to their own security. Lesser states are compelled to cluster under the shelter of neighbouring superpowers for security against the enemies they most fear, who are grouped in similar alliances. It is the decisions reached within, and above all between, these alliances that count. It is, in particular, the decisions of one or two superpowers – on weapons procurement and development, on the creation of a "strategic defence" system, on the abandonment of a previously agreed arms control treaty, on intervention in a third world state, in the final resort on whether or not to make use of a particular armaments system, such as nuclear weapons – which determines security throughout the world. Increasingly it is *international* security rather than national security which is the main object of concern. The entire world becomes a single political/military complex of which all the parts interlock. Purely national decisions on military matters thus become increasingly irrelevant. What matters to the inhabitants of a state is not the decisions reached on security by their own government but the decisions reached by governments or groups of governments elsewhere. Here too it is no longer national politics but global politics which count.

Many other issues, once felt to be the concern of national

governments alone, now become problems for the wider community. On many social issues the necessity of international rather than national action (and so of international rather than national political concern) is increasingly taken for granted. It is everywhere recognized that action against terrorists, or the hijacking of aircraft, has to be taken at a world and not a national level. The spread of AIDS and many other diseases cannot be prevented except by international action. The traffic in narcotic drugs cannot be halted by single governments acting in isolation but only by international measures. The care of refugees cannot be undertaken except on an international basis. The destitution of famine-affected populations can only be effectively relieved by international measures, rather than by a proliferation of separate national undertakings. The provision of financial assistance to poor, heavily indebted countries needs to be undertaken, not by competitive national programmes (often directed as much to promoting the interests of the donor as of those they are attempting to assist) but by international undertakings, especially those of world bodies such as the IMF, the World Bank or the World Food Programme. The twelve nations of the EEC join in establishing a "Social Charter", a programme of action defining social policies in all of them. Such examples could be multiplied. The rapid decline of distance, bringing general recognition of the need for international rather than national action, has the effect that on many questions of this sort the vital decisions – those, therefore, on which political controversy today must be primarily focused – are not the decisions reached by national governments but those that are reached internationally.

Action to safeguard the environment equally, increasingly insistently demanded in the modern world, can now only be effectively undertaken globally. For each individual citizen decisions reached on that question in other states are at least as important in their effect as are the decisions which are reached at home. Decisions designed to secure the safety of nuclear reactors in one country are of no value if its citizens are affected equally seriously by accidents occurring to reactors elsewhere, spewing radiation into the atmosphere which quickly crosses their own borders. The prevention of acid rain in one state is of no avail if acid rain from other countries continues to pour down, polluting lakes and destroying forests. The ending of marine pollution by one Mediterranian state is useless if industrial waste and sewage continue to be spilled into the seas by other states of the same region. Thus for ordinary citizens concerned about such matters the decisions which are reached within their own states are no longer those that matter. The political system within which those decisions are reached is altogether too puny and powerless to influence the outcomes which most affect them. If they wish to influence the decisions which matter most to them, therefore, only an influence on the decisions reached in other states, or by international bodies working in this field, will protect their interests adequately.

The need to prevent or reduce acts of repression and violations of human rights also now requires global action. For long it was enough for the citizens of each separate state to devote themselves to resisting such violations by their own governments: against themselves and their fellow citizens within that state. Opposition to such denials of rights became for long the major objective of political action everywhere: the principal demand for reformers and revolutionaries in every country of the world. Today concern about violations of human rights continues to be deeply felt. But it is now directed mainly at the oppressions which occur in *other* states. Those who no longer have great reason to fear gross tyranny and injustice in their own lands are today outraged about gross tyranny and injustice in others: arbitrary arrests, brutality, torture, imprisonment without trial, even the premeditated killing of those whose views and actions are politically inconvenient. Actions to express that concern – to influence, that is, the deeds of foreign governments towards their own citizens – can only be taken on an international basis: either by international pressure groups, such as Amnesty International, Survival and similar organizations, or by intergovernmental bodies, such as the UN Commission on Human Rights, or regional human rights organizations. Only these are likely to be influential enough to affect the activities of foreign governments. And it is, therefore, only political activity designed to affect those actions which can secure the political objectives most deeply felt by ordinary citizens.

But the irrelevance of action confined to the national political arena alone is seen above all in relation to the most fundamental political question of all: the distribution of power and wealth within society. It is that question which has been the most profoundly disputed and fiercely fought within national states, almost since such states began. It remains equally important today. But the main inequalities today, both in wealth and power, are not those within particular states. They are those within world society as a whole; not between the individuals of particular states, where inequalities have usually been at least marginally reduced, but between the most rich and powerful in the richest and most powerful states and the most poor and powerless in the poorest and least powerful states. It is these inequalities which now pose the principal challenge for political action. And it is the demand for action to reduce those inequalities, therefore, which is likely to be a dominant concern of politics – perhaps its main concern – in the years to come.

So, in many of the most important areas of political life, the traditional objectives and concerns can today only be adequately met by international action. The level of effective responsibility has risen above that of the individual national state. Economic management, security policy, important areas of social policy, the protection of the environment, the protection of human rights and the creation of a more just society, all of these are tasks which today can only be effectively undertaken on a global basis. Political activity designed to influence them must therefore equally be undertaken internationally.

Most individual citizens today are dimly aware of this growing interdependence among states. But they have scarcely taken in the significance of the change for political action. They are not yet aware that the political activities which they have traditionally undertaken are no longer relevant to the problems they now face, that the political parties they have traditionally supported cannot achieve the purposes that now matter to them, that wholly new kinds of political campaigning, new kinds of political organization, are now required. If international decisions are increasingly necessary, they tend to assume, this is a matter for governments to sort out directly between themselves. They are content to allow their own national government to seek the best arrangements possible to that end and trust them to protect their own personal interests adequately in doing so. They have yet to recognize a more immediate and personal interest in those decisions, and a duty to seek to influence them *directly*, comparable to that which governs their attitude to political action within their own state.

Current assumptions imply that their own interests exactly coincide with that of all their fellow citizens on each such question (so that the interests of all can be promoted by the actions taken on their behalf by their own government), yet may conflict with that of all the citizens of other countries. But in fact their own interests and that of their fellow nationals may be by no means identical. They may have a greater common interest with some of those who dwell in other states than with some of their own fellow citizens. On the way international security should best be safeguarded, for example, on what kind of weapons should be deployed and where and how, on what kind of arms control agreements can be concluded, there may be more agreement between themselves and some who live in other countries, about the same questions – supporters and opponents of nuclear disarmament, for example – than there is between themselves and many others who live within their own states. On the way the international environment should best be protected, on what should be done about acid rain or radiation from nuclear installations, they may find a greater community of view and interests between themselves and some citizens of other states than between themselves and many of their compatriots at home. On the protection of human rights elsewhere, they may have opinions more closely shared by some who live elsewhere, than by some who live within their own borders. And so on. On all these questions they may be a minority in their own state. And, even if they did have a majority of their fellow citizens on their side, they might still be unable, by influencing their own governments, to procure the decisions they demand. For that government, acting alone, is powerless. Only *international* political action – that is, action that is transnational, rather than intergovernmental, global rather than national – will be sufficient to bring about the objectives they desire.

The chapters below seek to explore the nature of this transformed political struggle in the principal areas where it is now beginning to be fought. It is a struggle which over time may increasingly overshadow, and eventually replace, the parochial political battles which still take place within states.

1 The Distribution of Political Power

THE CHANGING NATURE OF POLITICAL POWER

The principal concern of politics has always been with the distribution of power. Political thought and political action alike, whether seeking to justify and defend the way power is distributed at present, or to demand a new distribution to correspond with new conceptions of justice, welfare or efficiency, have each seen this as their central preoccupation.

The "power" with which they have been concerned has been that which was held within the individual state. It has been taken for granted that this was the political entity, the unit of authority, with which such discussions, or actions, must be concerned: if only because none other appeared conceivable. Humankind was organized in states; and it was therefore with the way in which power within states was managed that politics was concerned. The size of the state, the population which it ruled, the complexity of its administrative structure, might vary. But a state of some kind was, inevitably, the principal subject of political enquiry, and the proper arena of political endeavour.

Thus political action was devoted to maintaining or acquiring power within states. Religious leaders and secular rulers, kings and parliaments, aristocracy and bourgeoisie, peasantry and proletariat, struggled to win control of the levers of power by which states were controlled. Political organizations – factions, parties and pressure groups – were established at the national level for the purpose of waging that struggle. Individual politicians, seeking to win power for themselves, sought access to such national organizations. That focus of activity was logical and appropriate at a time when it was state actions, and therefore the control of state power, which determined the fortunes of all.

Political theory reflected that evolving struggle. Its doctrines mirrored, with remarkable faithfulness, the contest among competing classes, parties and groups to secure state power, providing the ideological superstructure for the contesting forces involved in the contest. The Republic of Plato, the Prince of Machiavelli, the

Leviathan of Hobbes, depicted different images of the way authority within the state should be exercised to the best advantage of its rulers or its population generally. Locke and Rousseau, Hume and Bentham, Marx and Owen, provided arguments to justify the dispersal of control within such states among wider and wider sections of the population. But, whatever the differences in their prescriptions for the exercise and control of power, none was in any doubt that it was state power that they were concerned with.

In the contemporary world this traditional concern of political thought and action has become of declining relevance. On the one hand, the progressive dispersal of power among wider and wider sections of the population, and the increasing reluctance of any to question the rightness of that process, has reduced the scope for controversy, or for striking new theories about the proper organization of political power within national states. Once a democratic system has been established, political debate and action have increasingly concerned questions of relatively marginal importance: the precise relationship between legislature, executive and judiciary, the details of parliamentary scrutiny and enquiry, the minutiae of the legislative or electoral process, the precise balance between the public and private sectors of the economy. The most important change in the way power is organized has already occurred.

At the same time the process of democratization has led to an increasing tyranny by the majority. This has brought a decline in the variety of the political prescriptions on offer. For none can diverge too far from what the majority is thought to desire. Political programmes, even those of opposing parties, become more and more alike. Socialist parties, which only fifty years ago offered programmes of full-blooded economic and political change – a radical extension of state power, massive nationalization and large extensions in welfare services, financed by substantial increase in taxation – now fear to offer anything more than marginal variations in the existing system, for fear of alienating the electorates to which they appeal. Conservative governments are not able, for all their rhetoric, to dismantle the welfare state, to reduce the generous medical and pensions benefits, or to cut back the high levels of public expenditure they once so vigorously denounced. Increasingly political controversy is confined to minor details of the organization of national life.

But there is a more important reason why traditional political concerns, related to the organization of state power, has become of less significance in modern times. This is that the power of states is itself far less than in earlier days. There is a paradox in this. On the surface the power of national governments in the modern world is greater than ever before. Their authority is less challenged within their own borders. Partly *because* of the process of democratization revolutions and civil wars are almost extinct activities in modern developed states. In any case the military power available to governments in those states now so far outstrips that available to any dissident group that such enterprises have no practical possibility of success. At the same time the authority of governments is extended, through an elaborate administrative structure, into ever more detailed areas of everyday life. The power of governments within their own territories, for all the efforts to constrain it, has thus never been greater than it is today.

Yet, despite all this, their real power is less rather than more. This is because, more than ever before, their capacity to control events, and to promote the welfare of their populations, is inhibited by events beyond their own borders. The most important developments which affect their populations are international events over which individual states have little control. More than in any earlier time the state, within which political activity has traditionally been concentrated, is not a self-sufficient political or economic unit, but only a fragment of a much wider entity: the world-wide political system, the international economy, world society. It is within this wider society that the important events now occur, that the major decisions are reached.

This affects every area of political life. It is not only that the military security of each state depends not on the decisions of their own government – about the level of its own armaments and the size and disposition of its own armed forces – but on external factors affecting international security generally. It is not only that the economic well-being of each state and its population is determined not by the economic decisions of its own government but, at least as much, by the decisions of other governments and international bodies, concerning rates of growth, commodity prices, interest rates, trade policy, investment, aid and debt: decisions which affect the entire world economy. It is not only that the ecological condition of each state is affected by developments that occur far outside it. Even more important is that the political situation within each country is increasingly determined by international factors: world-wide economic developments affecting the prosperity of their people; the influence of global political movements, such as international communism, Islamic fundamentalism, or Arab nationalism; the impact of foreign mass media, influencing the beliefs, the allegiance and the expectations of their populations; even in some cases by the direct intervention of external powers, which increasingly see political developments in neighbouring countries as of vital importance to their own security. World society becomes a single, interrelated political organism.

But there is another reason for the declining significance of national power in the modern world. In many cases the significant actors are no longer states at all, but transnational entities and forces which operate independently of states. In the economic field multinational industrial corporations now operate in a number of different states simultaneously, irrespective of national boundaries; and sometimes acquire a control of resources, and so of power, greater than that available to some national states. Transnational banks and other financial institutions, lending on a huge scale to many governments and corporations in many different countries, acquire substantial control over the economies of particular states, which become increasingly indebted to them. The most important actions affecting each country are often taken by these external forces. Churches and religious movements, world-wide political parties, cultural and social organizations, benefiting from the ease of communication made available by modern mass media, influence individuals scattered in a large number of different states around the world. Loyalties are no longer exclusively to the nation or to particular national governments. Often they are accorded to other, non-national, forces – ideologies, parties, movements, races, cultures – which influence the actions of individuals independently of the will of states.

These developments transform the nature of political power in the modern world. The autonomy of each state is progressively undermined. None is any longer effectively independent. Each is only a small part in a much wider process. The effect is that today the state is no longer the significant political unit. Political developments within a single country are little more important, in the framework of the wider political organism, than are political developments within local government areas in the framework of the national body politic. The political power that matters is no longer national but global power.

Changes that only affect political relationships within states have thus become increasingly marginal to the welfare of individuals. The only changes that are really important today are those that affect relationships *between* states; that influence those in other states who make decisions of key importance in international society. The basis of effective political action is thus wholly changed. The capacity of citizens, or of political organizations, to control the events that matter to them depends not on their ability to influence events within their own country, as in the past, but on their capacity to influence events in the wider world outside.

Modern politics, in other words, is global politics.

NEW CONCEPTIONS OF POLITICAL JUSTICE

This change in the fundamental entity of political life, the unit within which political activity takes place, has brought changes to other basic categories used in political discussion.

It implies changes, for example, in the conception of political justice. In discussing the distribution of political power traditional writers on politics have claimed to be concerned with the creation of a more just, as well as a more efficient, political system. What they have seen as just has varied widely. Plato was concerned with the distribution of power among men but not among women. Aristotle described the way political power might be distributed among citizens, but not among slaves. Hobbes was concerned with the right of citizens to choose their rulers, but not to control them. Bentham and Mill wanted an extension of the franchise to a larger number of citizens but not to all. Marx demanded political power for the proletariat but not for the bourgeoisie or the peasantry.

Many such writers, in seeking "justice" within the political system, were concerned to make political power more equal. Since power was often concentrated among small and privileged groups, political thinkers and actors alike demanded that it should be shared among a larger proportion of the citizenry. The exclusive enjoyment of power by particular groups and individuals was seen as an injustice to others who were subject to their decisions. So a great deal of political thought and action was directed to demanding, and securing, the extension of political power: from royal rulers to the great magnates who served them; from aristocracy to the bourgeoisie; from the bourgeoisie to the people as a whole. In this way, it was hoped, larger numbers would be enabled to protect their own interests through the direct exercise of political power. If *political* rights could be extended and equalized in this way, it was believed, the extension of other rights would follow. Political equality would be the means of securing equality of other kinds.

Some analysed the inequalities within society in terms of "class". In so far as groups and individuals were aware of inequality – that is of the difference in status, wealth and function dividing them from others within the same society – they would become "class-conscious": would see themselves, that is, as members of a particular group sharing certain common interests, as against those of other groups whose interests were dissimilar. Marx and his followers, in particular, saw this awareness of class, and the consequent struggle among different classes, as the fundamental factor determining change in society: the spur to political activity and so ultimately to the transformation of social relationships.

To some extent this was only a different formulation of the idea, widely accepted by political thinkers of all times, that differing groups and individuals are engaged in a continual struggle for political power as a means of promoting their own interests. The distinctive feature of the approach was that it saw *economic* factors as the ultimate determinant of "class"; and so of all political and economic struggle. Whatever the merits of the approach in the age in which it was conceived – an age of industrial revolution, when economic and political inequalities were at their most extreme and when no democratic means of securing political change existed in most states – its relevance to most contemporary national societies is limited. Though economic inequalities remain considerable in most developed states today, *consciousness* of those inequalities, and so of class, is everywhere declining. Repeated surveys of opinion show that, however deep the concern about inequality among radical political leaders and parties, among the majority of the population, including many of the most disadvantaged, it is slight. Repeated election results show that votes today are not primarily motivated by concern on that question (if they were, only socialist or communist governments would be elected). In such societies there no longer exist the extremities of poverty, among a sufficiently wide cross-section of the population, to determine exclusively political attitudes and actions. The progressive immiseration of the working population which Marx forecast has not occurred. On the contrary a steady increase in prosperity has been experienced by the bulk of the working population. The declining appeal of Marxist political parties and doctrine – indeed the decline of Marxist doctrine even among avowedly Marxist parties – is the clearest evidence of these changing attitudes among the populations of developed states.

Inequalities – sometimes substantial inequalities – continue to exist within each national state. But they are not so vividly perceived or so deeply resented as in earlier times. Because, however little the change that has occurred in *relative* positions all are to some extent better off, inequalities come to appear less important than other concerns, which are shared by many of the population and are unaffected by class factors: concern over the efficiency of economic management, the running of welfare services, environmental problems and the protection of individual rights. Increasingly, it is these which, in such societies, become the focus of political activity and political debate.

Yet this change has not occurred because inequalities, which have been at the centre of political debate for so long, and have been the most important single stimulus to political action, have been wiped from the face of the earth. Inequalities as glaring as any which have existed in any earlier time continue to exist. But inequality today, like politics, is globalized. It is world-wide inequality, both economic and political, rather than inequality within individual states, that is today most manifest and most unacceptable. It is the world-wide distribution of power which appears most inequitable. It is this, therefore, which has become of central political importance, and the focus of political concern. And it is *international* classes – and international class-consciousness – and not national, that are the main agents of political change.

International class-consciousness is related to the changing character of material inequality. The globalization of inequality can be demonstrated from the facts presented in Table 1. As this shows, the difference in income between the top and bottom quintiles of the population in Britain today is about 5.5 to 1. But the difference between the *average* income in Britain and similar countries and that in Bangladesh is about 40 to 1, and between the average income in the former and in Chad over 100 to 1. And the greatest, and most significant, difference between the top decile in Britain (or the US and Switzerland) and the bottom decile in Bangladesh (or Haiti or Buikina Fasso) is, of course, vastly greater than this.

In other words the significant inequalities of the modern world are not those that exist between different groups in the same state. They are those which exist between individuals in different states. If, therefore, the remedying of injstice remains, as it has always been, the most important single stimulus to political action and political belief, it is to the remedying of the injustices which exist at the international level that it will be directed. It is the inequalities between individuals in world society, not the increasingly insignificant inequalities which remain within individual states – whether rich or poor – that have become today the principal subject of concern to political thought and action.

Table 1 Relative Inequalities: National and Global

	Top quintile of households	*Second quintile*	*Third quintile*	*Fourth quintile*	*Bottom quintile*
National inequalities					
Percentage of final income in UK	40·0	24·0	17·4	11·8	6·7
Proportions (multiples of lowest incomes)	5·9	3·6	2·6	1·8	1·0
	Industrialized countries	*Developing countries*	*Low income countries*	*Bangladesh*	*Ethiopia*
Global inequalities					
Income a head (US $) 1986	12,960	69	270	160	120
Proportions (multiple of lowest income)	108	5·1	2·2	1·3	1

SOURCES: HMSO Social Trends (1988) p. 94; World Bank, World OECD, *Development Cooperation* (1988) p. 250; Development Report (1988) pp. 222–5.

The sense of injustice, which has always been the most important single stimulus to political action, and so the most important cause of political change, must today inevitably be focused primarily on injustice at the global level. For it is global injustices which have become the most visible and most widely resented.

THE DISTRIBUTION OF POWER IN THE MODERN WORLD

Political power means the capacity to secure desired political results. Nobody exercises absolute power. The power of even the most "absolute" and tyrannical rulers is always limited: by the extent of the territory they control, the loyalty of their armed forces and officials, the submissiveness of their populations. But within those limits the power of some is very great: they can secure most of the political consequences that are important to them. The power of others is almost nil: they are in most respects (even in the most "democratic" societies) always subject to the will of others – that is, powerless. It is differences in *relative* power therefore – in the degree to which individuals are in control of the events that are most important to them – that are significant. Such differences are inevitably closely dependent on control over resources: wealth, land, education, skills, health care and housing. Those who have the most control of these will usually have the greatest capacity to influence people and events.

It is differences of this kind – in control over resources, non-material as well as material – which continue to determine the distribution of power, political as much as economic, in the modern world. But the main differences of that kind today are not between those who live within the frontiers of the same state – though these differences can still be considerable, in rich and poor countries alike – but between those who inhabit different states. In the modern world the wealth, and therefore the power, of individuals is closely related to that of the state to which they belong. It is no longer mainly determined by individual abilities and aptitudes. Within each state, it is still possible to hope, the able and the industrious may be able to win success for themselves and their families, so that the *most* able and industrious can succeed most: secure the highest share of national income, the positions of greatest influence and so the greatest relative power within that state. But between states no such relationship can even be claimed to exist. However able and industrious the citizen of Bangladesh, whatever success he may secure within his own state, he will always remain less successful, less wealthy and less powerful than many, no more able and industrious, in developed states – often indeed, less successful, wealthy and powerful than many who have far *less* ability and aptitude in those states. Nor can he easily, because of controls on immigration, move to a country where he might secure a greater reward for his abilities. In other words the wealth and position to which any individual can attain is determined not so much by his own success as by that of the country into which he is born.

Among states themselves power is exercised overwhelmingly by the wealthiest and most advanced. These are the states which are mainly in control of political, as much as economic, events all over the world. It is the developed countries which, by their decisions on trade, debt, aid, rates of interest, the export of technology, the export of arms, sanctions, not to speak of direct military intervention where necessary, are able to influence political as well as economic developments in other countries all over the world. It is in the meetings among such states – for example in the Group of Seven, economic "summits" or the OECD – that many of the most important decisions affecting the world economy are reached: decisions that have as direct an impact on poor countries, which are not represented there, as they do on rich countries. Although in theory this imbalance in influence on world events might be counteracted, at least marginally, by the influence of other and more representative institutions – such as the United Nations and its agencies – in practice the role these play is insignificant. Precisely because they might seek to restrain the freedom of action of the most powerful states in the world, the latter increasingly ignore their actions and recommendations. They are bypassed by the major powers, who find it more convenient and fruitful to deal direct with each other, in superpower diplomacy and other more immediate contacts. It is in these encounters, involving only the most powerful states of all, that the most significant decisions, political and economic, of the modern world are reached. Control over events is therefore concentrated in the hands of a small number of powerful states.

Power in international society does not depend exclusively, any more than power in a national society, on economic factors. But the latter will always be of prime importance. If a country is poor, it will be militarily weak as well: it is unable to invest in the vast range of military hardware and advanced equipment that wealthier countries can acquire, and will thus remain militarily inferior to the latter. Even though it remains possible, because of political factors, for a very poor country – such as Vietnam – to secure military success against a very rich one, such as the US, it is not the case that such a country is therefore more powerful than the rich one. The US may not have been able to impose on Vietnam its will concerning the political system within that country; but Vietnam could still less impose its will concerning the political system within the US. If a country is poor it will also be technologically backward: it will be unable to spend on scientific education, research and development even a fraction of what can be spent by wealthier rivals. If a country is poor, its medical services will be inadequate, so that its level of health will be far lower. Its social services will be embryonic, so that poverty will be widespread. Its environment will be less well protected, so that the quality of life of its people will deteriorate. And so on. In other words, because it is poor, not only will the state be poor, but the life-chances of all its inhabitants will be more restricted than those of others, born under a different flag, elsewhere.

The distribution of power among individuals in the modern world is thus largely determined by the variations in the political and economic power of *states*. The control of individuals over events depends mainly on the power of their governments, which in turn reflects the national income and technological development of their countries. Because the US government is powerful, *all* Americans exercise, indirectly, substantial power in areas beyond US borders (however limited their power may be in the US itself). Because the Bangladesh government is not powerful, *all* Bangladeshis are weak in the areas beyond their shores (however dominant their role in Bangladesh itself).

Power in world society, in other words, depends not on who you are but where you live. It depends on the hazards of geography and history rather than skill, knowledge, abilities or any rational criteria. It is not relative personal income or personal position but relative *national* income and national position which is decisive. Whatever the degree of authority he may wield within his own country, the President of Bangladesh will always be relatively powerless in international terms. He and his country are dependent, financially, politically and technologically, on the decisions which are reached in other states. He is weak because his state is weak. The President of the United States, on the other hand, however much his power at home may be constrained by the checks and balances of the US constitution, in international affairs is invariably very powerful. He is powerful because his state is powerful.

If, therefore, the world has now become a single, closely interrelated political system, it is one in which the distribution of power remains, as in traditional political systems, highly unequal. But it is unequal not only as in the past, on the basis of occupation or class, qualifications or ability, but on the basis of geography. Thus a more rational or just distribution of power could be brought about not by political action taken within any individual state, but only by action that transcends geography: action, that is, taken within international society as a whole.

POLITICAL ACTION IN CONTEMPORARY WORLD SOCIETY

There are thus two related trends which have transformed the basis of political action in the modern world. On the one hand the power of individual governments is progressively reduced, as the actions and events which are significant to them and their populations come to be international actions, taking place outside their own borders, yet having a profound effect on them. On the other, citizens become more aware of the world beyond their national borders, which may affect their own lives. In particular, they become more conscious of global inequalities, in material conditions, opportunities and ways of life: since these now occur principally between states, and between individuals in different states, they can be effectively remedied only by actions at the international level. On this as on other questions the only type of political action which is significant is international action.

Both trends result fundamentally from a single cause: the reduced size of the modern world. That reduction in size has been faster in the last fifty or sixty years than in centuries before. The improvement in communications, which over previous centuries brought about the steady integration of substantial territories, including diverse regions, each having separate economies and differing ways of life, within unified national states, in the modern age begins to integrate diverse regions, economies and ways of life within the world as a whole. In travelling time the citizen of Tokyo is far closer to Washington and London today than the inhabitants of Manchester were to London a century or so ago. News, financial information, and visual images are transmitted far faster across the world than they were across a national state only fifty years ago. New social, political and cultural fashions, which might once take decades to spread even across a single country, can now travel across the earth in a few months. The shared *consciousness*, the sense of a common destiny, which is the most important condition of a single political culture, now exists within the world as a whole at least to the same extent as it did in most national states only a hundred years ago.

This has a profound effect on political attitudes. With the development of the mass media events occurring in one state become quickly known, and are vividly portrayed, to millions on the furthest side of the world. Only a century or so ago events in China could become known to observers in Britain only months after they took place. Even when they did become known the most cataclysmic events occurring there – a violent revolution, a famine, or disastrous floods causing hundreds of thousands of deaths – appeared so remote, both in time and place, that they could be of no immediate importance in the lives of the inhabitants of London; and anyway could not be influenced by them. Today a similar event – a student revolt in China, a famine in Ethiopia – is almost immediately known in every part of the world; will arouse widespread sympathy among populations elsewhere; and will induce rapid action on a world-wide basis, by individuals, governments and international organizations alike, designed to remedy the situation. The revolution in communications has brought about above all a revolution in awareness, in images of the world. In doing so, it has transformed the character of political action.

The change is at root a change in relative *visibility*. Events in other states become almost as visible as events in our own; and so a subject of equal concern. This transforms the effect of the new international inequalities already noted. What is politically significant is not so much the fact that the most extreme inequalities now occur at the international level. It is the fact that they are *seen*. International inequalities have become almost as visible as inequalities within states. In the past, although international inequalities were already considerable, and were known to exist, they were not the subject of mutual concern, as they are today, because they were less visible. The Manchester mill-owner knew of the existence of hungry Indian coolies. But they were not a subject of concern to him, still less of guilt, because they appeared to be creatures from another world. They were not his responsibility. The politician in Britain at that time might be genuinely concerned about poverty in various parts of Britain. But he was largely indifferent to that in other lands; for it was not visible to him, and was certainly not seen as his to remedy. A differential vision became established. This maintained a rigid distinction between problems occurring within the home country, which were the concern and responsibility of all who lived there; and those occurring elsewhere, which were not. Today, with the kind of global awareness which modern mass media create, such a differential vision cannot easily be maintained. The disasters which affect the Chinese student, the Indian labourer or the Ethiopian peasant are increasingly difficult to ignore. The duty to help avert them is hard to wish away. A global vision creates a global sympathy.

Equally significant, however, is the effect of the communications revolution on the vision of the disadvantaged themselves. For it is not only the comfortably off in the richer parts of the world who know more about the miseries of the disadvantaged in others. Those in other parts of the world are better aware of the more democratic political systems, the more productive economies, existing in richer countries. A century ago the Indian peasant, and those who spoke for him, saw and knew little of the life that took place in the great cities of Britain and the US. He scarcely knew that they were vastly different from his own. Still less did he conceive that he might aspire to them. Today he is only too well aware, from the television and cinema screens, of the standards of living and way of life which prevail elsewhere. He may even become conscious of the decisions, by foreign governments, transnational corporations or international organizations, which directly affect his own condition. This changes not only his attitude towards his own government and the policies it pursues domestically. It also affects his attitude towards the world beyond his borders. He too becomes increasingly aware of his place within global as well as national society. And he too gradually comes to understand that the injustices of the modern world can be remedied only by international rather than national action.

For the shrinking of distance affects not only the perception of the problems that are faced. It also affects conceptions of the means of changing them. It is increasingly recognized that national action alone cannot remedy the injustices that are most significant in the modern world; that political activity at the national level alone is thus irrelevant. Transnational political movements appear on the scene, concerned with securing changes at the international rather than the national level.

Some such movements have existed for more than a century. The communist Internationals called on the workers of the world to unite, to cast off their capitalist chains and create socialist societies. But they conceived this still mainly in terms of separate national revolutions in individual countries. These were left mainly to individual national movements to undertake, with little joint activity to bring them about. And such was the power of national consciousness that when their governments embarked on war in 1914, workers and unions and political parties nearly all supported their own governments in the conflict that ensued, while the International collapsed. After the success of revolution in Russia, the Comintern sought for a time to keep alive the hope of a widespread international movement for socialist revolution, led from the Soviet Union. But within ten years the leaders of that country publicly abandoned this objective in favour of "socialism in one country". Within another twenty years the Comintern was dissolved altogether.

It is only in very recent times that genuinely international political movements have begun to manifest themselves. Islamic fundamentalism, though it represents rather a simultaneous flowering of revolutionary sentiment in a number of countries separately than a single integrated movement, represents the most visible manifestation of this tendency today: the passionate concern expressed among large numbers, living in many different countries, for the transformation of the political and social system in other states as much as their own. President Reagan's "National Endowment for Democracy", dedicated to the spread of the system of government he favours, among many different countries, and his attempts, under the "Reagan Doctrine", to bring about direct changes in the political system in other states by assistance to revolutionary forces there, might be regarded as another manifestation of the same phenomenon. The Socialist International, bringing together democratic socialist parties throughout the world for the discussion of their common problems and endeavours, represents a further example of joint political activity on an international basis, though in that case with more modest ambitions and more restrained methods of operation.

These are mainly examples of international political action undertaken by individuals or political parties. But similar joint action is also increasingly taken by governments. Governments too today sometimes recognize that inequalities in power, both between states and between individuals in different states, can be rectified only by international action. Thus in the Bandung Conference in 1955 the governments of third world countries got together to assert their collective voice; and have since met regularly, in conferences of the non-aligned, expressing their viewpoint on most of the great political issues of the day. Often it is through decisions of international organizations that such groups seek to secure their aims. So the governments of developing countries have joined, in the United Nations and other institutions, in the so-called Group of 77 (now over 120), seeking to organize together to concert the positions they should take in the discussion of important economic issues. So, in the IMF, a group of 24 developing countries has been established with similar objectives in mind. So in many other international forums the governments of the third world concert together to maximize their ability to secure the political changes they demand. Rich countries, equally, act together to promote their interests: for example in the OECD, in which the most developed states of the world meet together to discuss their common economic problems and concert their policy; and in the regular "economic summits", in which the seven largest developed states meet regularly to discuss international political and economic issues.

More significant than either of these for the individual citizen is the development of transnational pressure groups, independent of governments. For long an important instrument of political action within states, pressure group activity now takes place increasingly at the international level. Because they recognize that many of the most important problems of the day require international rather than national action, such groups today organize themselves accordingly. So groups concerned about the environment form themselves into organizations as diverse as Friends of the Earth, Greenpeace, the International Institute for Environment and Development, and world-wide ecology groups, to battle, within international organizations and national states alike, for more enlightened policies. So disarmament groups – CND, END (European Nuclear Disarmament) and others – are formed to campaign for disarmament not in one state but in many. So human rights groups, such as Amnesty and very many others, increasingly organize at the international level as much as they do at the national. Organizations of scientists, economists, doctors and parliamentarians form themselves into world-wide associations, often campaigning on specific issues. On a large range of the most important political questions of the day, international movements and associations now exist to promote particular interests and viewpoints on problems which are increasingly recognized as international rather than national.

Nor is it only those who demand radical change who organize themselves in this way. Those in positions of economic power equally – large industrial companies, banks, chambers of commerce, associations of manufacturers and employers – now organize themselves internationally, to protect their interests. On the one hand, the activities of each, with growing size, extend across borders, so that they become "transnational" organizations, operating in large numbers of countries throughout the world and often even "multinational", based in several countries (if only to be able to minimize their tax burden). On the other, they group together in associations of manufacturers of particular kinds, chambers of commerce and other bodies, to be able to represent the interests of their members in a world where the decisions which most affect them are reached in a wide range of different countries and international organizations. Trade unions become linked in comparable transnational confederations. They too recognize that in the modern world they increasingly need to be in a position to exercise influence beyond their own states and in the wider world beyond. For them too politics is globalized. Essential interests, which could once be protected only by action undertaken in separate national political systems, can today be protected only by action within the international system as a whole.

Finally, the process of institution-building also becomes international rather than national. A substantial part of political action and thought has always been devoted to the building of institutions: to establishing political structures which could more effectively, or more justly, fulfil the functions believed to be most important by the political actors and thinkers of the day: better law-courts, more representative parliaments or more efficient government machines. This too is a task which is increasingly transferred to the international level. Though the process of modifying and refining national political institutions will continue to take place, the changes made in that way within states become increasingly marginal. The main challenge, and the main demand for change today, comes increasingly at the world level. It is above all changes in international institutions, therefore, which are demanded to fulfil many of the functions seen to be important, by individuals as much as to states. It is above all through changes in those institutions that political power may come to be more widely and fairly distributed than it is today. The struggle for a more just sharing of political power, so long the centre of all political activity, will become above all a struggle concerning the future of world political bodies.

The relevant unit of political activity today is thus no longer the national state but the world political system. It is changes in the latter rather than in the former to which effective political activity is likely to be devoted. And it is to an examination of the way that struggle is likely to be undertaken in particular areas that we shall turn in the chapters that follow.

2 The Safeguarding of Security

THE END OF NATIONAL SECURITY

For centuries political discussion has been concerned with the means of preserving the citizen against threats to security, external and internal. That task was seen by many political philosophers (for example by Machiavelli) as the central task of the state; even (for example by Hobbes) as the initial reason for its foundation. The supreme duty of governments, many practical politicians believed, was to undertake those tasks effectively.

It was a function which, until recently, national governments appeared fully capable of undertaking. It was not beyond their power, it was felt, to build up their armed forces, to organize their defences, to enter into alliances, if necessary, to safeguard their territory and populations. By such means, it was expected, their peoples might be protected from the ravages of war and the destruction of house and home. They would even, as a result, have little direct experience of the trials and tribulations of warfare: those hardships would be mainly confined to the armed forces, whose specific task it was to protect the security of the state and of individual citizens within it.

Today there is not a single state, not even the most powerful of all, which can claim to be able to safeguard the security of its population. Modern weapons technology has transformed their capacity to do so. A hundred years ago the mass of the population in every state lived far beyond the range of even the most powerful weapons its enemies could dispose of. Today the entire population of every state, however remote the areas in which they live, are within range of powerful missiles which, even if stationed many thousands of miles away, can strike directly against them. A hundred years ago the most powerful warhead available to an enemy was a heavy artillery shell, capable of killing a dozen or so men, supposing that they were unfortunate enough to be victims of a direct hit. Today the most powerful warheads are capable of destroying the populations of entire cities at a blow, and even conventional bombing raids – as on Dresden and Tokyo in 1945 – can kill 100,000 in a night. A hundred years ago, however rapidly armed forces were mobilized and however quickly an army was rushed to the battle-front, it might take weeks to capture an enemy city, and a month or even years to reach its capital. Today the destructive power that is available can be delivered to the furthest points of an enemy's territory within minutes. A hundred years ago, the casualties of war were mainly confined to servicemen, and most weapons were specifically designed for use against them. Today, the types of warfare employed and the weapons used, whether nuclear or conventional, guerrilla or terrorist, are likely to cause almost as many casualties to civilians as to military personnel.

In such a world no government can provide security for its people. The entire concept of "national security" has become obsolete.

That change began many decades ago. The strategic autonomy of individual states has been declining for a century or more. In the latter half of the last century the spectacular defeat of states seeking to defend themselves alone and single-handed – Austria in 1866 and France in 1870 – brought a new recognition of the vulnerability of individual states operating in isolation. This was reflected in the formation of alliances, which were no longer, as in earlier days, short-term and opportunistic arrangements, to be quickly abandoned when no longer convenient, but relatively stable features of the international system: such as those between Germany and Austria of 1879 and between France and Russia of 1893–4. By the early years of this century even Britain, which had previously long prided herself on her "splendid isolation", was willing to join in understandings (though still not in alliances) with her former antagonists, France (in 1904) and Russia (in 1907), to provide greater security against the country that she now saw as the principal threat to the peace of the continent. Even the US, which throughout her history had sought to avoid "entangling alliances", in 1917 became willing to joint with other states, even in another continent, against their opponents (as she was to do again a quarter century later). National security, it came to be realized, might demand the defence of other countries as well as one's own.

In the inter-war period the inability of many states, especially smaller states, to safeguard their own security against larger and more powerful neighbours became even more manifest. A succession of nations and territories were rapidly swallowed up by expansionist powers, employing bitzkrieg tactics for the purpose. So Manchuria, Ethiopia, China, Austria, Czechoslovakia, Poland, and eventually most of the other states of Europe, fell one by one. No "guarantee", as provided to Poland and Rumania, nor even bilateral defence pacts, as between France and Czechoslovakia, proved of any assistance to them. The speed of military movement was now so great that a state could be overcome and occupied long before any effective assistance could be provided from elsewhere.

This was the lesson that was learnt in the years after 1945. If individual states could no longer provide for their own security in 1939–45, they were still less likely to be able to do so in the years to follow. Increasingly, in east and west alike, and in every other part of the world as well, neighbouring states joined together in relatively close-knit "treaty organizations" or pacts, providing for a far greater integration of their military capability than any of the "alliances" of earlier times had done (which had normally provided no significant degree of military cooperation in peacetime). More and more it was now explicitly recognized that no country in isolation could provide for its own security. Effective security, it was accepted, depended on the close cooperation of a number of states acting together.

Yet, with the advances of military technology, it was soon discovered that such alliances were no more able to provide security than individual states had been able to do in the age before. However many allies a nation might boast, however closely it integrated its forces with theirs, it was still vulnerable to death and destruction rained from the skies at any moment. A number of new developments had destroyed the basis on which the concept of "security" had been based.

First, the increasing range, speed, and sophistication of missiles meant that there was no longer any part of the national territory which could be defended. Since the largest missiles now had a range of 12,000 miles, they could reach virtually any point on earth. Since they were now housed in moving platforms, such as submarines, aircraft in flight and mobile launchers, they could not be immobilized by a disabling first strike. Since they could be launched in very large numbers, at considerable speed, and with many decoys, no realistic means existed (not even, most scientists believed, the much-vaunted US Strategic Defence Initiative) which could prevent them from reaching their targets. Since the delivery of even a single warhead, for example on major cities such as New York, London or Moscow, could cause millions of deaths and virtually immobilize a nation, the emergence of such weapons threatened not simply the "security" of the state but its entire existence. And since the radiation from such weapons would be quickly spread (like that from Chernobyl) over a large number of other countries around, the concept of "national" security was now particularly inappropriate: the state which employed such weapons would threaten its own population as much as its enemy's. It was no longer national security, nor even "Western" security, but *international* security, the safety of all who lived within entire regions of the earth, on either side of the east–west border, that was placed at risk by such weapons.

Nor would the risk be very much less if nuclear weapons were not employed at all. The power of modern conventional weapons, it was now apparent, was only a little less. They, equally, had destroyed the capacity of individual states to provide for their own security. Missiles bearing conventional warheads only could, with all the advances and refinements in such explosives made since 1945, wreak destruction on a vastly greater scale than the already hugely destructive bombing raids of the Second World War. Chemical weapons, employed with little compunction in Vietnam, and sporadically in other recent conflicts, could cause casualties as great in scale as nuclear warheads. Biological weapons, though theoretically banned (like many other weapons subsequently employed in war), would cause far more. Other modern weapons – particle beam and kinetic energy weapons, lasers, cluster bombs, anti-personnel mines, "smart" weapons of various kinds, electronic guidance mechanisms of increasing sophistication, rocket artillery, these and many others less publicized, could cause casualties, among civilians and servicemen alike, on a scale infinitely beyond those experienced in the Second World War (estimated at nearly fifty million). The distinction between the destructiveness of nuclear and conventional war was thus far less than was often popularly supposed.

The technology of modern warfare had destroyed the concept of national security in another way. The speed of military movement now possible meant that entire national territories were placed at the mercy of neighbouring powerful states. Soviet forces were able to occupy Hungary and Czechoslovakia in a day; US forces could occupy Grenada in a day or so. One effect was that the "defence" requirements of a state now stretched far beyond its own borders. The US saw the defence of Western Europe, the Caribbean, Central America, and even (it was at one time said) South East Asia, as essential to her own security. The Soviet Union saw the control of Eastern Europe and Afghanistan as essential to hers. Thus the defence needs of a whole group of countries were increasingly merged. The Eastern European states were incorporated in the defence requirements of the Soviet Union: they were unable to provide for their own defence interests independently of those of the Soviet Union. Central American states were seen as part of the US's defensive perimeter: they were not able to conceive of their defence needs independently of the political and security interests of the US. The days in which a state could think in terms of a purely "national" defence were long past.

There was, finally, yet another reason why the idea of national defence had become obsolete. The main threats to security no longer derived from the traditional sources: major assaults across frontiers by the arrayed armed forces of another state. Warfare was increasingly undertaken not for territorial but for political purposes; and it was undertaken normally by non-conventional means: guerrilla warfare (as in Vietnam, Afghanistan, Nicaragua, Angola, El Salvador and many other places today), or by terrorists (as in Lebanon, India, Sri Lanka, Northern Ireland, Spain and elsewhere today). In either case the traditional means of preserving national security became irrelevant. In guerilla wars even the most powerful conventional forces (such as those of the US and the Soviet Union) were unable (as events in Vietnam and Afghanistan proved) to prevail against well-organized guerilla forces. Such forces were thus no longer able to protect what had been held to be vital national security interests. Terrorist organizations operated on a transnational basis, threatening simultaneously the security of a number of different states (if only marginally); yet they themselves were not clearly rooted in any one and could be countered, because they operated internationally, only on an international basis. In both cases the outcome of such struggles depended on political rather than military factors: factors which were often themselves international rather than national in scope and character.

New ways therefore needed to be developed to preserve the security of citizens against new types of threat, which were now frequently political rather than military, international rather than national in scale.

Traditional notions of national security had become irrelevant. In the security field, as in so many others, the national state was no longer adequate.

THE FAILURE OF COLLECTIVE SECURITY

If individual states were no longer capable of maintaining security for their populations, the obvious way of protecting them was by the development of some system under which nations would act together to defeat any attempt by another to disturb the peace.

This was the aim of the system which was established for a time in 1918 and revived, for an even briefer period, in 1945: the system of "collective security". It was essentially a more sophisticated and highly organized form of the balance of power system which had operated for centuries before. The balance of power system, though often derided by those who proclaimed the collective security ideal, was in its heyday devoted to the same objective. It was based on the presumption that it was necessary, if order in the European continent was to be maintained, for states to combine against whichever other nation represented the principal threat to the peace at any one time. In conformity with that principle most of the states of Europe had joined to defeat Louis XIV in the Nine Years War and the War of the Spanish Succession; several joined against Frederick the Great in 1756; and nearly all did so (at different times) against France in 1793–1815. Even in the nineteenth century, though for long there was no single power which was obviously the principal threat, the principle to some extent operated. There was some joining of ranks against France in the years after 1815 and after her adventure in Italy in 1859; against Russia in 1854–6 and after her victory against Turkey in 1877–8; and above all against Germany when she increasingly became the dominant power and the main threat to peace in the early years of the following century. But the persistence of particular enmities (for example between Austria and Russia) or particular friendships (for example between Germany and Austria) had the effect that for much of this time the main aim was to establish a "balance" in the modern sense – that is a rough equilibrium of power between particular states and groups – rather than a "balance" of the kind previously understood – a favourable balance mobilized against the major threat to the peace at any one time.

The system in any case failed to maintain the peace of the continent. It was only with the establishment of the League of Nations in 1918 that "collective security", in the sense that the term came to be generally understood, was put into practice. Under that system the peace was supposed to be maintained not by *ad hoc* alliances against any state seen as a threat, but by a permanent alliance of the overwhelming majority of peace-loving states against any particular state which might at any moment threaten the peace. Every member of the system committed itself to "preserve as against external aggression the territorial integrity and political independence" of other states. In place of a precarious "balance" of power, a decisive *preponderance* of power was now to be mobilized against any state which refused to accept a peaceful resolution of any dispute in which it was engaged.

If resolutely and consistently applied, such a system might have been able to preserve a peaceful world. But there were sufficient loopholes to ensure that, if resolution was lacking, it would not operate in the way intended, and aggression would not therefore be restrained. In practice, whenever a crisis arose, all could find plausible reasons for inaction. Since no state was under a binding obligation to send armed forces to come to the aid of a victim of aggression, all found excuses for not doing so when an attack took place (as when Japan seized Manchuria in 1931 and Italy Ethiopia in 1935). Even economic sanctions were only once employed, and then hesitantly and incompletely, against Italy in 1935–6 (a number of states declining to participate and the most significant commodity, oil, being altogether excluded).

There were other weaknesses in the system. It was not collective in the full sense, since the organization which operated it was never universal. The United States was never a member. Those states which were most interested in challenging the status quo – Japan, Germany, Italy and, eventually, the Soviet Union – were only members for a few years. Collective security was thus never put into effect. Successive aggressions were not deterred. And on its final culmination in 1939, aggression was countered only by the responses of *individual* states, defending what they saw as their national self-interest, not by any collective decision of the organization as a whole.

Thus, at that war's conclusion, when the United Nations was set up, it was designed to create a more reliable form of collective security. In this case the "teeth" which the League had lacked would be provided: in the form of a Security Council force which could be called on to confront an aggressor state if necessary. In this case all the major powers of the world would be members; and the most powerful of all would be accorded a privileged position as permanent members of that Council, so that they could together cooperate in maintaining world peace. In this case the obligation of member-states to come to the defence of the state under attack would be made more compelling, through an explicit commitment to obey any "decision" of the Council that they should take such action.

But there was no real improvement. Though in appearance an advance on the League's inadequate system, the new provisions proved in practice equally inoperable. The proposed Security Council force was never established. The major powers would not agree to cooperate in maintaining the peace of the world. On the contrary they used the organization primarily as a means of attacking each other. They rarely agreed on what should be done in individual cases. The obligation of the members to come to the aid of a victim of attack was never even put to the test. It began to be reluctantly recognized that the willingness of states to take such action, whatever pledges they had made in signing the Charter, was limited. In the only case which could reasonably be called a collective security action, that in Korea in 1950–3, the call for assistance to South Korea was therefore made in the form of a recommendation, rather than a mandatory "decision". And it was heeded by only sixteen states, states which might have taken such action anyway in the defence of their own purely national interests.

The belief that peace could be maintained by a system of "collective security", a belief that held sway among many for thirty or forty years after 1918, was based on a myth. It depended on an optimistic faith in the willingness of states to see the defence of another country, even if situated at the furthest end of the world, of differing political beliefs, culture and way of life, as so essential to their own interests that they would take up arms on its behalf. That faith was a delusion. It grossly overestimated the degree of public-spiritedness to be expected of most member-states of the international system. No such willingness existed. States would join with their immediate neighbours in defensive arrangements to protect their common security interests. They would not fulfil an abstract commitment to regard the defence of every other state of the world as essential to their own, regardless of ideology, cultural and political affinity, or geographical distance.

So it was not "collective security" therefore but "collective defence" that was now put into practice: the establishment of rival alliances, the members of which were committed to assist each other in the event of attack on any one. In this case it was more reasonable, because of their close association, to expect each member tc regard an attack on one as an attack on all. Even if they could not maintain the peace of the world as a whole, such arrangements might at least preserve the peace for the limited group of states that belonged to them. Because a potential aggressor would know that it would not be able to undertake a private act of force against an individual state, but would need to confront the combined strength of all the members of an alliance together, attack might be deterred. In this sense at least the internationalization – or at least the regionalization – of security was recognized. Within a limited area the defence of one became the defence of all.

A confrontation of rival alliances of this kind was closer to the balance of power system as it had been practised at the end of the nineteenth century (for example in the confrontation of the German–Austrian and Franco–Russian alliances) than to a collective security system in the modern sense. It helped preserve the peace of Europe (apart from intra-bloc upheavals, in Greece in 1946–9, in Hungary in 1956 and Czechoslovakia in 1968) reasonably well for forty years. But it could not, for a number of reasons, provide genuine security over the long term.

In the first place it was essentially a bipolar, confrontational system rather than a genuinely international one. It could preserve the peace so long as each side frightened the other sufficiently to deter it from attempting any action which might disturb the peace. But if one side failed in that aim (as the *Entente* powers, at a time of similar confrontation, failed to deter Germany and Austria in 1914) such a system would fail in its objective. Nor could it deter acts of force *within* the area controlled by either of the alliances: for example Soviet intervention in Hungary and Czechoslovakia in 1956 and 1968. Nor could it prevent domestic conflicts, taking place within a particular state rather than between them: such as the Greek civil war of 1946–50. Still less did it deter the uses of force that had now become most common: armed action undertaken outside the area immediately covered by the alliances, such as successive US interventions in South East Asia and the Caribbean, or Soviet bloc interventions in Africa and Afghanistan. Above all, because it could not, like the collective security system, establish a *preponderance* of power against any threat to the peace, but only an unstable equilibrium which might at any time be disturbed, it was by no means certain that it would continue to deter, even in that limited sense, indefinitely.

For there was another reason why such a system might prove unstable over the long term. Deterrence was maintained, on one side at least, by an assertion that even an attack undertaken by conventional forces only might be met by a nuclear retaliation. But that was an assertion of rapidly declining credibility. In the first two or three decades after 1945 such a threat was not an altogether incredible one. Nuclear weapons had, after all, been used in that way – that is in a previously conventional war – only a few years earlier. So long as the western powers maintained some kind of overall superiority in nuclear armaments and means of delivery, it might therefore still be believed that they would be willing to use them against a conventional attack, just as they had been used against Japan only a few years previously. But as soon as the Soviet Union, from the early seventies, acquired something like an equivalence of power, that threat became incredible. It was no longer possible to believe that, whatever they might say – for deterrent purposes – western powers were willing to commit suicide by precipitating what was certain to become an all-out nuclear exchange, and expose their own territories as much as their enemy's to nuclear radiation (Chernobyl had made only too clear that radiation would not obligingly remain on one side of a border only) in response to a purely conventional attack. In practice, whatever they might say in advance, they were always likely to refrain from a response to a conventional attack which must almost certainly bring about the destruction of all their major cities and the loss of much of their population. This must be only too apparent to their enemies. It thus meant a return to a purely conventional balance of power. It was therefore no longer inconceivable that incidents might once more occur which could, in certain circumstances, lead to an attempted use of force by one side or the other, and so to a highly destructive armed conflict, even if one fought with conventional arms alone.

But there was a third change in the international situation, more important than either of these, which had the effect that collective defence alone was increasingly incapable of maintaining international security. Those arrangements were intended to meet the kind of threat that occurred in 1939: an all-out assault across national boundaries by an enemy in Europe. But the conflicts which occurred in the post-1945 world were entirely different. They did not take place between the two rival alliances at all. They occurred entirely outside the area which was covered by those arrangements: in Asia, Africa and Latin America. Most of them occurred only *within* individual states, rather than between them. Though developed countries sometimes became involved – above all the superpowers – in providing armed support to one side or the other in such a civil war, or at least as suppliers of arms, they were never directly involved against each other. The balance of power between them, therefore, whatever influence it might have in deterring a direct confrontation in Europe, was irrelevant in its influence on the type of conflicts that did now occur, or even on external intervention within them. Their incidence, their severity and their outcome were none of them in any way affected by the arrangements for collective defence made within the Euro-Atlantic world. Those arrangements may indeed have if anything intensified conflicts elsewhere. The stalemate in Europe meant that the East–West rivalries were exported to other parts of the world. The conflict which they did not dare fight out, with all the terrible means at their disposal, in Europe was pursued, with bitter intensity, in other places. The entire globe became the battlefield for a vast political struggle. The intensity and bitterness of that struggle was in no way deterred by the truce imposed in Europe.

But not only did collective defence arrangements fail to deter conflict between the superpowers and their allies in the areas outside Europe. They provided no security whatever for those, the great majority of the world's states, which inhabited those areas: the very states the security of which was most precarious. The great majority belonged to neither of the main alliances. A few engaged for a time in regional collective defence arrangements, promoted by one side or the other (for example in Cento and Seato); or in bilateral agreements with superpowers or former colonial powers. But these were of no assistance in the type of conflicts in which they mainly became engaged. Threats to security now came mainly from domestic rather than external sources: from political instability, often intensified by economic failure and administrative weakness. Factional conflicts of that kind, often of an ideological character, were likely to be intensified rather than contained by the rivalry of external powers, each eager to assist their own political protégés. And they were certainly not influenced by collective defence arrangements undertaken among the more developed countries of the world to meet their own, purely local, security requirements.

Collective security and collective defence alike, therefore, were unable to provide stability for the greater part of the world. The entire globe had now become the battlefield. Security had become, more than ever before, indivisible. The mutual confrontations of rival defence pacts provided, even in Europe, only a precarious security; and elsewhere, in the areas where war was endemic, none at all. Still less did the abstract commitment to a system of "collective security" – an empty promise, virtually never fulfilled, to come to the assistance of any other state that was threatened – provide any safeguard.

Only a quite different approach to the security problem was likely to be effective. What was required was a genuinely collective approach, as neither "collective security" nor "collective defence" had been: that is a fully international system. It needed to cover the world as a whole, as contemporary regional defence arrangements did not. And it needed to be based on *mutual* understandings concerning security – multilateral arrangements rather than bilateral threats – if it was to be able to provide any genuine measure of security, for states and individuals alike.

ARMS CONTROL AND DISARMAMENT

Traditional methods for improving international security – both the balance of power and collective defence arrangements – had depended on attempts to establish some kind of balance, whether an equal balance or a favourable balance, to deter or defeat aggression. The effort to negotiate agreements on arms control and disarmament were based on a similar hope. Whether arms were held at existing levels, as in arms control, or agreed reductions were brought about, as in disarmament, the aim was to ensure that there existed a rough equivalence, so that no state was tempted to believe that it could secure its aims by exploiting any advantage in available armed power in its own favour.

If an agreed balance of this kind could indeed have been secured, it would doubtless have helped to create a greater sense of security among states. But all such efforts suffered from two serious difficulties. They underestimated the problem of securing agreement on what represented a balance; and they overestimated the advantages which would be gained even if such an agreement could be arrived at.

The difficulties of securing understanding on what constitutes a balance would be serious enough even if the balance was one to be established between two contestants only. There are obvious difficulties in comparing, and so balancing, different types of armed strength: missiles of varying size, range and accuracy, with and without independently targetted warheads, mobile and non-mobile, sea-based and land-based; between aircraft of differing speed, range and manoeuvrability; between tanks of differing fire power, armour, speed and horsepower; highly trained regular forces and less trained conscript forces; forces that are held close to the front (such as Soviet forces in Europe) and forces which are held further away (such as US forces based in the US); so many warships (for a sea power) against so many battalions (for a land power); and so on. There are a wide range of *qualitative* differences, which are even more difficult to measure. Technological advance has the effect that even similar types of weapons may vary widely in sophistication and effectiveness. Even slight differences in the age of almost identical weapons may influence their utility. Agreement on numbers alone therefore, even if it could be secured, would not resolve disagreement of this kind.

Such difficulties are made still greater when (as is inevitable) consideration is given not to individual states but to entire alliances. What is the weight to be attached to varying numbers of allies of differing national incomes, size and power; devoting different proportions of their national income to defence expenditure; some possessing nuclear arms some not? Should an equal weight be given to the forces of east European states, sometimes held to be politically unreliable, with west European forces, believed to be better trained and more highly motivated? Should allowance be made for the special responsibilities of particular allies: for example, for the defence of overseas territories; or for the length of the frontiers to be defended (a factor brought into the argument during the interwar disarmament negotiations); or the need for a defence against a wider range of possible enemies (such as the need for the Soviet Union to be prepared against possible opponents in the Far East as well as in Europe); and so on. Should the aim be to bring about exact *equivalence* between two alliances, or should account be taken of the differing populations, or the differing number of countries in each?

But in fact consideration cannot be confined to alliances in isolation. For example, the Soviet Union cannot be expected to negotiate reductions in its armaments that take account of the level of Western armed strength but not of that of China or Japan. Similarly, China cannot be expected to negotiate substantial reductions in her armed strength unless India does so too. And India cannot be expected to do so unless Pakistan does likewise; in which case Pakistan may demand reductions from Afghanistan and Iran as well. And so on. In other words the balance which is ultimately needed is not between two alliances only, but one which is world-wide. Such a world-wide balance, given the varying number of potential enemies which each state has, is likely to be so complex as to be unattainable. It is, for example, logically impossible to discover a balance which matches the forces of NATO with those of the Warsaw Pact, but which also matches the latter with those of NATO and China combined; or which matches the forces of India and China, but also allows India parity with China and Pakistan combined. As these examples show, it is not possible even to begin to discuss appropriate balances without making political assumptions about the likelihood of conflict between particular states and groups of states in the future: calculations which are likely to give rise to almost insuperable disagreements.

But this complexity is still further intensified by the fact that the situation is not a stationary one but a dynamic one. Even if it could once be agreed, no balance is likely to be immutable. A change of alliance by one state or another would radically alter the equilibrium achieved and so require some compensation to be made if the balance was to be maintained. New technological advances would continually disrupt the balance, and would then stimulate further efforts by opponents to redress it once more. Unless technological change were to be halted altogether – which is inconceivable – no state could be prevented from improving its military potential as a result of technical advances: for example in the field of computing, electronics, aeronautics, rocket technology or laser developments, among many others.

There is always at least one state which believes it is catching up with an opponent in one or more fields, and will demand time to close the gap before it will agree to stabilization. Sometimes both sides may simultaneously believe themselves to have a need to catch up (as at the time of the alleged "missile gap", or at the present time with strategic defence research). Because judgements about the existing balance are made on the basis of subjective judgements, each side – above all its armed forces – tends to inflate the advances which have been made by its opponents and believe that it still has more ground to make up before a balance can be achieved. Given such competition only agreements which have little military significance (such as that relating to intermediate missiles in Europe, leaving 97 per cent of nuclear weapons unaffected) are likely to be attainable.

Again, there are the problems which arise about how an agreement is to be controlled and verified. When the question is only of large-scale installations (such as missiles) the problem – with modern satellite surveillance – is reasonably manageable. But if the desire is to balance warheads, the most destructive element in existing military capabilities, the problems are virtually insuperable. There is no system of verification conceivable which could provide foolproof evidence that no warheads had been kept concealed, above or below ground, in the vast territories of the two superpowers (one reason why warheads are not affected by the intermediate missiles agreement). It is thus not realistic to think of agreements that could, reliably and incontestably, establish a "balance" in the total destructive power held by the two sides. If this, the most destructive element in the armouries of both sides is to remain untouched, it is unlikely that disarmament agreements of any type will do much to promote mutual security.

This leads to the second of the difficulties described above. Even if all the problems already enumerated had been overcome, and it had proved possible to achieve, by some miraculous stroke of a magic wand, a world-wide agreement, covering all arms, all countries and all combinations of countries (not an easy outcome to imagine), what would have been achieved? Unless a supra-national force had at the same time been set up, equipped with armed power sufficient to coerce every individual state – in other words a form of world government established – the balance established could not be maintained on a permanent basis. Nothing could prevent any of the 170 or so parties to the arrangement at any time repudiating the agreement, resuming the manufacture of arms, nor from subsequently making war against an opponent. If only limited disarmament agreements had been achieved in particular fields, as is more likely, it would be still simpler to abrogate the agreement as soon as it became no longer convenient (as the US has recently done with SALT II). Indeed whatever agreements may be negotiated in the future, it remains overwhelmingly probable that, whenever a major international crisis occurred and tension once more became acute, such agreements would be abrogated in that way by one or more states. And once it had been abandoned by one, other states would follow its example. In other words, agreements of this kind may *consolidate* the mutual confidence that already exists (in which case they are not needed). But they are of little value in influencing the actions of states, or their willingness to go to war, when that confidence no longer exists (the time when they are most required).

In a world in which armed power is held in the hands of individual sovereign states, in frequent and sometimes violent conflict with each other, it is inevitably difficult to arrive at understandings about mutually agreed levels of armaments in the first place. But it is even more difficult to ensure that such states will afterwards unquestionably maintain such undertakings at times when tension is high and suspicions easily aroused about the intentions of opponents.

The underlying problem is that such questions, like all the other problems relating to international security, are still viewed through the eyes of national or alliance decision-makers, engaged in a continual competition with their rivals, representing other states, each viewing the scene in an equally self-interested way. A dominant voice in determining policy in such discussions is given to representatives of the armed services: those who are most inclined to see the proposals of their opponents with suspicion. The question is therefore looked at through 170 different pairs of spectacles, concerned above all with 170 separate national security interests. Only if the matter were viewed under a perspective less distorted by the partial vision of national self-interest, might a different type of solution be sought. Then it might be seen that the question was ultimately not one of national security at all, but of *international* security: a problem which cannot be confronted by individual governments in isolation, nor even by rival alliances in competition, but only by a common effort to confront the security problems of international society as a whole.

THE INTERNATIONALIZATION OF SECURITY

The citizen looking for security can no longer, therefore, look to the national state to provide it. Neither states in isolation, nor alliances of a number of states, are able, acting in mutual competition, to provide security for their citizens.

The attempt to obtain security by unilateral means – whether by states or alliances – is based on a logical fallacy. It is based on the belief that each party can maximize its own security by maximizing the *insecurity* of its opponents: that is, by ensuring that it remains in a position, if necessary, to destroy its rivals. But that threat compels the opponent, if only in self-defence, to maintain a similar threat in reverse, and so to develop an equivalent destructive capacity. Each, therefore, imposes insecurity not only on the other but on itself. Since neither side can acquire a guaranteed defence against attack by modern missiles, whether nuclear or conventional, neither can altogether remove the threat held by the other. No state, nor any alliance, can any longer therefore (as in earlier times) obtain for itself the superiority which would provide some assurance against its own destruction. All remain equally vulnerable.

Even parity, with which both main alliances are now content, provides no security. An ability to prevent the other from prevailing does not provide safety for oneself. In any future nuclear conflict, whichever proves victorious, both sides equally will be destroyed. A policy based primarily on mutual threat is therefore self-defeating. The only result is that both sides remain permanently insecure. The objective shared by all governments – to provide security for their own citizens – is thus defeated. States (or alliances) which all equally desire security, all win equal insecurity.

Unilateral policies, designed to maximize the threat posed for others, might make some sense if such hostility existed between two states or alliances that they were incapable of communicating with each other to discuss more rational policies. It might then be reasonable to believe that, because he was inaccessible, an opponent contemplating war-like action could be deterred from this only by the fear of instant retaliation. The policy might then be a rational one even though it involved constant insecurity for all. Even in those circumstances it might be a mistaken one. For the very fact of the threat, by increasing the sense of insecurity, might make an opponent more, rather than less likely to consider aggressive action. The threat posed against him might lead him to believe that, whatever his own intentions, those of his opponent were hostile. And this could lead to the use of defence strategies, weapons procurement policies, precautionary measures of various kinds, troop movements, and, finally preemptive military action, designed to forestall military actions against him, or to establish a commanding military position at the outset of hostilities. At a time of crisis, mobilization orders, "red alerts" and other steps, even if intended by each side as defensive, might be taken by the opponent as the prelude to full-scale war, and stimulate him to corresponding counter-measures. Mutual threats – "deterrence" – may thus, instead of being a force for stability as intended, be a powerful force of instability. They may serve to provoke the very actions they are intended to prevent.

But if the opponent's motives are not aggressive, then security policies based on threats are still more irrational. For they may only prevent the more peaceful relationship which both sides desire from being established. By implying mutual hostility they deter mutual understanding. The threat which one party deliberately poses makes it necessary for the other to adopt a military posture in response, which in turn deters any relaxation of attitude by the first. Eventually each may cease to attribute peaceful motives to the other. One side or the other may then convince itself – however irrationally – that it can defeat deterrence: that it can, for example, by a preemptive first strike, eliminate all its enemy's missiles in one fell swoop; or undertake a large-scale conventional attack without fear of nuclear retaliation because the opponent fears nuclear war as much as he does; or take offensive action without risk because he has developed a "strategic defence" system capable of overcoming all incoming missiles. Such assumptions, none of them inconceivable, destroy the basis of mutual deterrence. A policy of mutual deterrence depends on an assumption that opponents will be prudent and rational. And so long as each side does indeed behave rationally, and has no serious war-like intentions it may work well. But in that case it is not necessary. It is precisely because it is only an irrational act which is likely now to result in full-scale war that strategies based solely on mutual deterrence – and the assumption of prudence and rationality – are insufficient.

Thus if major war has not occurred between East and West since 1945, it may not be, as widely believed, because of successful deterrence. It may be simply because neither side has had sufficient *motive* to undertake an expensive external war of the old-fashioned kind. Deterrence has not prevented military action *within* their spheres of influence by both superpowers: including military actions within Europe where the confrontation is at its closest. However unacceptable the actions taken by the other side – in Vietnam as in Afghanistan, in Grenada as in Hungary – opponents have not thought of intervening to oppose them (so that, while the failure to defend Czechoslovakia in 1938–9 was widely regarded as a disgraceful act of appeasement, the failure to defend Hungary in 1956 and Czechoslovakia in 1968 were regarded as acts of statesman-like restraint). But it can never be certain that similar prudence will always be shown in the future. In time governments may come to power on either side which no longer exercise a similar restraint – which may, for example, no longer fear that nuclear weapons might be used in response to a purely conventional attack – and which therefore fail to be "deterred" by existing policies of mutual threat.

The underlying reason for the danger that still exists, and may become more serious in future, is that security policy at present is still *unilaterally* devised and executed: not by single states but by individual alliances acting competitively. It is for this reason that each side seeks security for itself by maximizing insecurity for the other: so in practice creating maximum insecurity for both. The maximization of insecurity for both parties is only likely to cease if policies come to be multilaterally devised. Such policies would be directed not at one-sided security but at mutual security.

If such a change were to come about, and if as a result negotiations were genuinely to seek a cooperative rather than a confrontational approach towards security questions, and to seek multilateral rather than bilateral solutions, what would be the specific types of measure which would be aimed at? The first, and minimum, requirement if the risks of one-sided security policy are to be reduced, is improved *communication* between the principal antagonists. It is the lack of communication which at present breeds magnified suspicion of the intentions of opposing parties, overestimates of their warmaking potential, and misapprehensions about their intentions. At present it is above all better communication between East and West which is required. This is not altogether lacking. It takes place to a limited extent through diplomatic contacts, ministerial and summit meetings, negotiations on disarmament and arms control. Mutual understanding is improved, marginally, by the "confidence-building" measures which are already undertaken. It may be improved further if mutually agreed measures for verification of disarmament agreements are established. But for the purpose of reducing risk and improving stability, these are not sufficient. It is above all on the type of strategies and weapons-procurement policies employed that there is the greatest need of further understanding. And it is here that at present communication remains minimal; deterred above all by mutual suspicion.

If it is the case, as seems probable, that neither East nor West at present has the deliberate intention of aggression against the other, each side has an equal interest in the adoption of strategies, deployments and weapons systems which reflect that fact; and which will therefore reduce the risk that either side may misjudge the intention of its opponent and seek a preemptive strike, whether limited or comprehensive. The fact that offensive capabilities are deployed at present does not mean necessarily that either side has offensive intentions. It results from the philosophy that attack is often the best means of defence; and because it is by no means easy to distinguish between strategies and weapons whose purpose is offensive and those that are defensive. Of course both sides continually declare that, though the aim of their opponent may be aggressive, their own is purely defensive. But so long as they accompany these words with warlike preparations, including manifestly offensive weapons, the words are not necessarily always believed. The simplest way of reducing mutual suspicions would be by the adoption of arms control policies and strategies which matched the words: which were, that is, clearly defensive rather than offensive in purpose. The aim would still be to achieve a balance; but a balance between armed forces demonstrably deployed in such a way as to minimize the apparent, *immediate* threat posed to an enemy (even if still maintaining the ultimate threat of instant and powerful retaliatory action were the other side to take the initiative).

If *mutual* security became the aim it would be accepted that armaments should be deployed in a way which represented the least provocation to the opposite side and was least likely to arouse the misplaced fear of offensive intentions (and so stimulate preemptive action). This might reduce the problem (pp. 29–32 above) of agreeing explicit measures of arms control and disarmament. The problem would become one of securing a qualitative, rather than a quantitative balance. So long as the aim is to ensure that both parties (or all parties) hold equal numbers of missiles, bombers, battleships and countless other categories, there will continue to be difficulties of the kind described: about the equivalence to be attributed to different types of missiles and other armaments, having differing ranges, accuracy and penetrative power; about the levels of armament to be accorded to allies; about verification; as well as about the balances which would be created with non-parties to the agreement. But if negotiations were directed not to the *numbers* of arms of different types, but to the *types* of arms which were held, these problems would be eliminated, or at the very least reduced.

If it was agreed that future weapons procurement would be confined to arms generally recognized as defensive rather than offensive in intention – to be defined by agreement – the exact number of those weapons held by either side would become less significant. The important thing would be that the degree of threat the armaments posed would be reduced. Thus security would be increased, not for one side only, but for both. Reductions and measures of control might be concentrated on those weapons – tanks, bombers, air-to-ground missiles and mobile armoured units – which were primarily offensive; while leaving untouched those types – anti-tank weapons, interceptor fighters, ground-to-air missiles and ground forces – which were primarily defensive in character. The security of each side would be maintained. But the perception of threat would be reduced.

In the same way, if *mutual* security became the objective, the aim would be to avoid dispositions and strategies which were provocative and destabilizing, and to adopt those which were stabilizing in their effect. This distinction might affect policies both in the period before conflict had erupted and after it had begun.

In the pre-conflict period the objective would be to take all possible steps to reduce the likelihood of misunderstanding, hasty responses, abrupt mobilization; above all a decision to undertake "anticipatory self-defence" by either side. This would require a commitment to the maximum restraint at moments of high political tension; and the creation of command systems which ensured that no decisions could be taken by local commanders which could fatally commit either side to an excessive response. It would require arrangements providing for the maximum communication, not only through hot-lines between heads of governments, but between commanders in the battlefield, enabling misunderstanding to be rapidly corrected and confidence established. It could require the establishment, by mutual agreement, of systems for command, control, communications and intelligence which ensured not only that both sides retained control of operations within their own area and so were able to maintain effective restraint where necessary, but that they refrained from disrupting their opponent's system and so inhibiting the necessary communication, including cease-fire initiatives. It could require a prior agreement on the procedures to be followed by both sides in the event of an incident: an aircraft straying off course, or even civil disorders within their opponent's sphere of influence (perhaps the most likely trigger for an unintended war). Steps of this kind would go far beyond the types of confidence-building measures that have been discussed so far between the two alliances (for examples, in the context of the Conference on Security and Cooperation in Europe).

But it is above all the strategies to be pursued *after* major hostilities have begun which need to be most carefully considered if the dangers are to be reduced. To assume that once war has begun all peacemaking efforts have failed, and that nothing more can be achieved, is a doctrine of despair which could have calamitous consequences. The difference, in contemporary conditions, between a conflict that was carefully limited in its scope and cost, and one which was unlimited, including an all-out nuclear exchange – in other words, the end of most civilized life on earth – is so vast that it is above all at this stage that effective measures to secure restraint are needed.

The most obvious immediate objective would be to limit the geographical area of the conflict. That aim was successfully achieved in the Korean and Vietnam wars – the two most serious East–West conflicts of the post-war period. In both cases there were strong pressures in some quarters for the wars to be extended – to the

Chinese mainland and to North Vietnam respectively – steps which would have vastly increased the cost of both struggles; and in both cases those demands were successfully resisted. This is the type of war-limitation that is probably the easiest to implement, since the distinction involved – based on geography – is the most clear-cut. It is one which will be particularly necessary in any future conflict in Europe. Since such a war is unlikely to take the form of a *general* assault by either side across the East–West border, but might emerge from a more local cause (say a civil war in Yugoslavia, a confrontation in Berlin, a frontier incident in Turkey or a *coup d'état* in Greece), there would be both the opportunity to establish geographical limitations of this kind and a clear need to do so. The chance of securing such restraints – even after a conflict has already begun – is far greater if the need for them is clearly recognized in advance and the means for negotiating them established.

The same applies to restraints in the type of armaments employed. Some such restraints have been observed in most wars of the recent past. Gas was not used by any party in the Second World War. Biological weapons have never yet been employed. Nuclear weapons have been renounced in all wars since 1945, even when (as in Vietnam) they might have been thought to make all the difference between victory and defeat. Over recent years it has been generally concluded that no explicit renunciation of nuclear weapons can be made by the Western powers, because, it is believed, they represent a unique deterrent against war of any kind, nuclear or conventional. In fact their capacity to deter conventional war is now minimal, since it is no longer credible that the major Western states would expose their cities and populations to total obliteration in seeking to resist a purely conventional attack (which would almost certainly have only a limited objective); and even less credible that such weapons could be employed, at however low a level, without leading relatively soon to an exchange of nuclear weapons of all kinds. The maintenance of this unbelievable threat thus weakens rather than strengthens deterrence, since it could give rise to a belief – however false – that, because of the excessive reliance placed on it by Western states, the latter would in practice prove unable to meet a conventional assault effectively. An unequivocal declaration that NATO will avoid the use of such weapons – except against a nuclear attack – would therefore not only limit the possible scale and cost of any future war in Europe – to the benefit of both sides – but, by restoring the credibility of deterrence, make such a war less likely.

There are a number of other types of measure which, once questions of security were discussed on a cooperative rather than a confrontational basis, might prove to be mutually acceptable. For example, both sides might accept that there was an advantage (to both) in a reduction in the level of armaments, or even in a general demilitarization, in the areas immediately adjacent to the front lines between them. Since it is from these areas alone that any offensive action could be undertaken, a thinning out or an elimination of forces would be the clearest evidence of peaceful intentions on both sides, and would do most to make clear that an attack would be unsuccessful (since much greater warning would be provided of it if that intention should change). In a further and wider area beyond the front line limitations might be placed on the *type* of armaments that could be deployed: for example prohibiting not only nuclear and chemical weapons but the more offensive types of conventional arms, such as heavy tanks. Such areas could be made subject to continuous mutual inspection, both to prevent violations, and to give advance warning of any offensive action if it were to be taken (again reducing the possibility and advantage of surprise attack). Arrangements like those already made – for the notification of troop levels, troop movements and manoeuvres – could be extended to a still wider area; and made more comprehensive so that, for example, exceptions for "alerts" and mobilizations (as permitted at present) which largely nullify the utility of the measures, were no longer allowed. More intensive efforts could be made to arrive at agreed estimates of existing levels of arms held by all countries, and inspection introduced to verify these: this would eliminate the instabilities which result frequently (not only between East and West but, for example, between Israel and the Arab states or between India and Pakistan) from exaggerated estimates of the armed strength of other states. Finally, understanding could be sought on the proper role and limits of strategic defence: how far it may be stabilizing in its effect, as when undertaken for specific missile sites (as in the ABM Treaty) to increase their invulnerability; and how far it is destabilizing when attempted for the whole of a state's territory (as under the Reagan Plan), by awakening the fear that the ultimate intention is the creation of a first-strike capability.

It must be recognized, however, that all the agreements we have described, even if they could be reached, would be of strictly limited value. They can be effective only if the intentions of both sides are anyway peaceful. If those intentions change, if either side, or both, decided for whatever reasons to seek to promote their interests through war once more, then all the understandings previously established would be thrown aside: demilitarized zones would be reoccupied, prohibited weapons would once more be acquired, and war might once more become a possibility. In other words, agreements of this kind can maximize and enhance the degree of mutual confidence which already exists. They cannot create it where it does not exist.

But there is a second and more important reason why agreements of the kind outlined are of strictly limited value. For they guard principally against the type of conflict which is anyway increasingly unlikely: an all-cut armed confrontation between East and West in Europe (it is even arguable that such measures have become possible only because that type of conflict has ceased to be in the interests of either side). But they could have little influence on the type of conflict which does still occur, which does correspond to the interests of major powers and which remains the chief danger to world peace: competitive interventions in conflicts outside Europe. The type of action undertaken in those places, the type of armaments employed, and the areas where they occur, would be altogether unaffected by any understandings of the kind we have described: for example, for a reduction in levels and types of armaments, for demilitarized zones, or even for systems of mutual inspection in Europe. For the kind of activity which is most widely undertaken today a totally different type of understanding would be necessary.

Again the first need would be to promote communication between the major centres of power, above all the superpowers, which become involved in such conflicts. In that way some understanding might be established concerning the main concerns and interests of either side in the areas in question. Since the roots of nearly all such conflicts are political – that is, they concern the competition for political power among rival factions in particular states – it is above all over the political aspects of each struggle that understandings would be necessary. Those understandings might need to relate to the political processes by which such a conflict could be resolved. And they might provide the basis for mutual self-denying ordinances, under which all would agree to refrain from intervention.

More general understandings might be designed to outlaw all external intervention in such conflicts. Ground rules might be established concerning the degree and type of assistance which might be provided in civil wars without undermining the basis of world order: what type of arms and supplies might be provided, to which parties, in what circumstances; what should be the role of the United Nations or other international bodies in seeking solutions. It is in such cases that the need for a collective rather than a competitive approach, for multilateral rather than unilateral action, is especially manifest. For often it is precisely the lack of such an approach, the competitive and uncontrolled character of unilateral intervention, which makes the situation so dangerous. While over the immediate East–West confrontation in Europe there is an increasing measure of mutual good will and an increasing willingness to keep within well-established ground rules, in the conflicts of the third world no such understanding exists. It is here that the danger of unintended confrontation is highest. And it is conflicts of that kind – as in Korea, Vietnam, Afghanistan, Nicaragua, Angola, Mozambique and many other places – which have been the most destructive and dangerous of the post-war world. It is about these above all therefore that the need for a collective rather than a competitive approach is greatest.

Those conflicts are not merely threats to international security, resulting from the external intervention they invite. They are, more directly, threats to the security of the inhabitants of those countries themselves. Over 20 million people are believed to have been killed in conflicts of that kind since 1945. In many cases the level of casualties and destruction has been hugely magnified by the intervention of powerful outside states, backing one faction or another. It is the people of that country, therefore, who have the most direct interest in the establishment of procedures which could minimize their costs. Most begin at least as civil conflicts, resulting from contests for power in particular states. What is most required therefore are procedures that reduce the temptation to resort to arms in such situations. This can be done only by establishing political, in place of military means, for resolving the contest for power: for example by the institution of internationally supervised elections to resolve the conflict and (if possible) the establishment of democratic systems in which legitimacy of governments is difficult to challenge.

If competitive *national* interventions designed to determine the outcome of such conflicts are to be deterred, it is more effective intervention by international bodies which is needed. We shall consider in Chapters 7 and 8 below the improvements in international institutions which a global political system requires. In the particular area we are here concerned with, that of security, the need for such improvements is especially evident. If international influences are to become more powerful in relation to national, then United Nations bodies need to play a more prominent role than they do today. The detailed negotiations about strategic arms reductions, strategic defence, intermediate missiles and such-like will still need to be conducted between the states which possess such weapons. But the negotiations they undertake may still be usefully influenced by the pressures of international bodies. Those bodies provide a voice for the uncommitted, and so a place for the synoptic vision of outsiders. That more objective view is sometimes needed, to influence and guide the more committed positions of the principal participants. International fora can also provide the means to promote contacts and communication between adversaries, and so reduce mutual suspicion. Finally, they are needed to define the general principles which should underlie the disarmament process and the wider system of peaceful coexistence.

Discussions of security at present, even when undertaken between alliances, are undertaken by national decision-makers, affected with the narrow viewpoint, partial and partisan, of national government representatives. They are there to represent their state, or at best a group of states, and to promote the interests of these to the best of their abilities. There is no representation of non-state actors, of non-government political parties, of non-governmental organizations, still less of the mass of humankind as a whole. In a few cases neutral states take part and may inject a somewhat less partisan note into the proceedings (as Sweden, India and Nigeria have sometimes done in the Geneva disarmament negotiations). But their influence is minimal. In general the interest of the *individual* in security – international security – goes by default. It is only the interest of the *state* – in national security – which receives expression and determines the course of the discussions.

Even within governments the national viewpoint is mainly determined by defence departments. These express an attitude which is usually, if not bellicose, at least highly mistrustful of potential opponents, and wary of any proposal which they believe may reduce their own country's war-making potential. The primary concern of such representatives is with ensuring that their own states will secure a successful military outcome if war were to occur; how to defeat the enemy, how to foil a surprise attack, how to destroy the enemy's forces. Even if their advice is in theory based on the assumption that the object is to prevent a war rather than to fight it efficiently, their inclination is inevitably to assume that only the latter will achieve the former. In such a framework the interests of the citizen in security – international rather than national security – is likely to go by default. It is the interests of the *state* in national security, as defined by itself, which determine the course of the discussion.

Individuals have an interest in security which is independent of that of their states: an interest in international rather than national security. Only if non-state actors were able to influence such debates, directly or indirectly, would that interest be adequately recognized. This would demand the establishment of international pressure groups and parties and international sources of advice and information, able to compete and challenge that which comes from governments. Already today such bodies as the International Institute of Strategic Studies, staffed by experts from a number of different countries, and not representatives of governments, play a significant role in influencing and modifying the partial judgements on security questions made by the representatives of national governments. The Stockholm International Peace Research Institute (SIPRI), based in a neutral state, and explicitly committed to reducing the burden of armaments, represents a more radical source of influence and an alternative source of information or opinion on such questions. Movements such as the international "freeze" movement, and the European Nuclear Disarmament movement, with a membership that comes from both sides of the iron curtain, can also represent genuinely international viewpoints which may encourage their governments towards a broader and less partisan view of their own national interests and those of their people. At present, however, such movements and institutions are relatively weak in their influence. And they are representative of only a small proportion of the world community, based in western Europe and North America. To be able to influence international discussions towards a genuinely international view of security, far more broadly based and politically influential organizations would be required. And they would need to acquire a more direct impact on the negotiations that take place than they have today.

If the security requirements of a closely interrelated world are to be more adequately met, it can only be by seeking to discover a broader and less partisan view of what security entails. Sometimes this broader view can be promoted by the representatives of third parties, those states not themselves involved in any particular confrontation, which can inject a more dispassionate and impartial viewpoint than that of the parties themselves. Sometimes it can be promoted by international officials and intergovernmental bodies, having a responsibility which goes beyond that of the national state and embraces the world as a whole. But it can be provided, above all, by those who do not represent states at all: international pressure groups, non-national institutes, above all the mass of ordinary human beings whose security interests are at risk when such questions are discussed, yet at present have little opportunity of expressing a view. Since it is their security which is ultimately involved, it is they above all who should be given the opportunity of influencing, more directly than they can today, the course such negotiations take.

What is at stake in such discussions is not the security requirements of individual governments, nor even of individual states. It is the common security needs of individual humans. True security will be discovered only through collective action to create a collective good: by seeking to promote, not the separate security demands of individual states, but the security requirements of mankind as a whole.

3 The Promotion of Welfare

THE GLOBALIZATION OF WELFARE

The safeguarding of their citizens' security is not the only task which national governments, acting individually, can no longer undertake effectively. They have also increasingly assumed responsibility for guaranteeing to their citizens security of another kind: protection against material hardship. This too in modern conditions, they have found, has increasingly required to be undertaken within a wider framework.

From early times it has been accepted that one of the duties of governments was to protect the material interests of their citizens: in particular, to safeguard them from total destitution. This was reflected in the actions of medieval European monarchs who, by restricting exports and promoting imports, by prohibiting altogether the export of grains and other essentials, and by encouraging foreign merchants to bring their products to their markets, sought to ensure that essential supplies, above all of foodstuffs, were available in home markets; the so-called "policy of plenty". Arrangements were sometimes made for the provision of food to the needy in time of famine or harvest failure: it was one of the duties of justices of the peace in England in Tudor times to undertake this. Minimum levels of wages were often laid down by statute. In some countries special arrangements began to be made to safeguard the livelihood of the most disadvantaged of all. In England, under the Elizabethan poor law of 1598, parishes were obliged to provide "necessary relief for the lame, impotent, old, blind and other such being poor and not able to work". "Overseers of the poor" were appointed to supervise the relief and to provide work for those capable of working. Local parishes could be taxed to provide the funds that were necessary. This remained the essential mechanism for relieving poverty in Britain till 1948.

The extent of the relief provided was scarcely generous, and was modified from time to time. At the end of the eighteenth century the arrangements were for a time amplified so that even those in employment could have their wages supplemented to ensure their livelihoods: relief was adjusted to the size of the family and the extent of their needs. But that system was soon abolished and the availability of poor law relief was significantly reduced during the 1830s when, though there was certainly no reduction in need, there was a general presumption that work could be found by those who needed it, in the cities if necessary, and that no relief was therefore required for able-bodied men, however many dependents they might have.[1]

The general principle that public provision must be made to help those in the most severe hardship continued to be accepted, however. With the growing authority and resources of national governments, the responsibility for providing assistance began to pass upwards from local authorities to national states. New groups of disadvantaged were found who needed to be assisted. Before the end of the century support for the elderly, previously obliged to rely on the support of their immediate families, began to be provided: old age pensions were introduced from the 1870s in Germany, and in many other countries during the following fifty years. Measures were introduced to protect the rights of children (for example in the Custody of Children Act introduced in Britain in 1891). Widows' pensions began to be introduced (from 1925 in Britain). Special protection was provided for low-paid workers in particular industries where it was difficult for them to organize effectively, such as catering and agriculture: trade boards to protect their interests and regulate wages were established (from 1909 in Britain). During the depression of the inter-war years the unemployed became another group for whom special help was needed and, at least on a limited scale, provided: in many cases this was now done both for the insured and the uninsured, often with special allowances for children (though at very low levels and usually subject to means tests). Finally, after the Second World War, the range of benefits which national governments provided was rapidly extended and a significant proportion of national income came to be redistributed in transfer payments of one kind or another.

Thus the "welfare state" became the main instrument for reducing inequalities and alleviating hardship. It was taken for granted, as in the case of defence, that it was the state – that is the national state – which was the appropriate instrument for undertaking that task. From this point the scale of the responsibility states assumed for that purpose continually increased. Social security became the largest single item in most national budgets.

But, by a paradox, the more successful each state became in providing for the needs of their own populations, the more the original purpose for which these measures had been designed, the

1. See Maurice Bruce, *The Coming of the Welfare State* (London, 1961) pp. 32–56.

relief of the very poor, ceased to be achieved. The more effectively each state dealt independently with the problems of poverty within its own borders, the less effectively disadvantage was remedied world-wide. For poverty is always essentially a relative concept. What appeared as extreme poverty in a rich country might appear affluence in a poor one. Destitution, in the sense which had been understood in earlier centuries, increasingly ceased to exist in rich countries. True destitution, the risk of starvation, which traditional welfare measures in rich countries had been designed to relieve, now occurred only in very poor states. Yet those were precisely the states which did not have the means to provide the relief that was necessary.

This was not, however, the only reason why the promotion of welfare had become a task beyond the scope of individual national governments. In some cases the reason that a disadvantaged group could only be helped by those outside their own state was not because their own government was not *able* to help them, but because they had no *wish* to do so. In such cases only cross-border activity was capable of assisting them. This had been the case, for example, for slaves in earlier times. When consciences began to be pricked about the existence of slavery two centuries ago, concern began to be expressed most eloquently in states where slavery anyway no longer existed. It was not difficult for Denmark to pass legislation abolishing the trade in slaves in 1802 since it had no slaves and few slave traders. British governments were active from 1815 in promoting international action to stop the trade in slaves; but they did not abolish slavery in British territories until 1833. But legislation by these European countries, even when it occurred, had little effect on the continuation of the practice in those states, in the Americas, Africa, and Asia, where slavery was still widely practised. To influence the practice of other states international action was required. So it was that the Treaty of Vienna included a declaration by the signatory governments committing them to abolish the slave trade; and so it was that eventually, in 1890, sixteen nations committed themselves in an international convention not only to terminate the slave trade from their territories but to establish international supervision to ensure that this was effectively undertaken. Eventually, therefore, a world-wide international movement, and the world-wide action that resulted, was able to bring about the abandonment of the practice itself throughout most of the world.

A similar situation occurred over the protection of fundamental labour rights. Although individual governments had begun from the first half of the nineteenth century to protect their own industrial workers, through measures limiting hours of work, especially for women and children, and enforcing more rigorous safety measures, such steps were of no assistance in preventing exploitation in other countries whose governments had not chosen to take similar action. During this century concern at such practices in other states (especially if they were competing states, such as Japan) became more widespread. At the end of the First World War another major peace treaty therefore provided for international measures to disseminate acceptable standards. The signatories committed themselves to take part in joint action to raise the conditions of employment all over the world. They were to join in establishing a new international organization, including representatives of trades unions and employers, to ensure that the rights of workers were effectively safeguarded. So all members of the League (as well as one or two states which never became members of that organization, such as the US) joined in creating the International Labour Organization, with responsibility for laying down the standards to be preserved. These were set out in a series of international conventions. New machinery was established – providing for the cross-examination of representatives of each ratifying country – to ensure that the standards – relating to hours of work, safety at work, the right to organize trade unions, the right to reasonable wages and conditions, the right to be free of discrimination or arbitrary dismissal, for example – were effectively observed.

So international standards were laid down to ensure equality of treatment. In other cases only international bodies could undertake the task required because no single government was capable of dealing with it. After the Second World War, for example, one of the most severely disadvantaged groups on earth were the millions of people that were driven from their own countries by the ravages of war, famine or oppression, and had been obliged to flee to the shelter of another country. But that other country could not always provide for them the assistance they required. It might have neither the food, the accommodation, the manpower, or the other resources necessary to take care of the often unwelcome immigrants. Only international action could therefore provide the welfare services needed. So it was that a series of international organizations – the International Refugee Organization (IRO), the United Nations Relief and Rehabilitation Administration (UNRRA), the UN Works and Reliefs Administration, with special responsibility for Arab refugees (UNWRA) and the UN High Commission for Refugees – were established with specific responsibility for providing the assistance, including shelter, food and in some cases education, which no national government was able or willing to provide.

In other cases international action was necessary because of the increased ease of travel in the modern world. This created new problems which no individual government in isolation could deal with. For example, there was increased danger that infectious diseases, often transmitted by travellers, could be passed rapidly from one country to another. Only concerted action, including the rapid notification of an epidemic, the modification of travel arrangements, the requirement of vaccination certificates, and other types of cooperation could cope with such a crisis effectively. World-wide campaigns might be necessary to eliminate a particular scourge; like that undertaken in the case of smallpox, and attempted for malaria. Sometimes research coordinated on an international basis was required to confront some new threat: as in the case of AIDS. Or international regulations and conventions might be necessary to bring about the abandonment of practices, originating in some countries but affecting others; such as those concerning the sale of baby milk products or the safety of medicines generally. To carry out these and other necessary measures of protection new international bodies were created, both at the regional and the world levels: above all the World Health Organization, which became the principal body responsible for action in this field.

Increased mobility brought other problems requiring an international response. After the First World War a flourishing international traffic in prostitutes stimulated international measures to cope with it, for example in the League's Committee on the Traffic in Women. After the Second World War, the traffic in narcotics produced still more intense international cooperation, including the establishment of new bodies, such as the Commission on Narcotic Drugs, and the UN Fund for Drug Abuse Control, to maintain an overview of the world traffic in drugs and coordinate the action of governments against it. The internationalization of criminal activity of many kinds made necessary the establishment of the International Criminal Police Organization (Interpol) to coordinate and supplement the activities of national police forces while the UN organized consultations on criminology and legal practices. The development of international terrorist organizations in the sixties and seventies made necessary closer cooperation among the interior ministries of different countries and new international conventions to ensure effective joint action against such activity. In other words problems relating to law and order and the elimination of crime, traditionally the responsibility only of individual states acting independently, now increasingly made necessary international counter-measures.

Thus, just as, a century or so earlier, social problems which had previously been confronted only at the local level, within the family and the local community, had increasingly been made the responsibility of national governments, so now some of those problems had to be confronted on a still wider basis. Many had become global rather than national problems. Crime, drugs, terrorism, disease, refugees, national disasters, had become matters which individual governments acting in isolation could no longer effectively cope with. They were incapable, above all, of dealing with the most serious social problem of all: relieving the situation of the most disadvantaged – the totally destitute – since in most cases these lived within those states which were themselves most disadvantaged and least capable of helping them. If such problems were to be confronted at all, this had to be done at a level above that of the state.

THE POLITICS OF WELFARE

Though national governments had undertaken an increasing measure of responsibility for relieving poverty, doubts about the need or scope of action were expressed from the beginning.

When the poor law was first introduced in England, there were some who feared that public assistance might undermine private responsibility and sap the spirit of self-reliance. Sir Walter Raleigh declared that "hunger and poverty make men industrious"; and so implied that their relief might make men lazy. The puritan ethic, extolling individual enterprise and seeing self-help as a sign of inner grace, deplored excessive reliance on charity, private or public. "If thou be upright and diligent in thy lawful calling," William Perkins, the divine, wrote at the beginning of the seventeenth century, "thou shalt finde sufficient for this life"; for this reason public provision should be unnecessary. At the beginning of the eighteenth century, Daniel Defoe, in his pamphlet, *Giving Alms no Charity*, declared that "the reason why so many pretend to want to work is that they can live so well with the pretence . . . they would be made to leave it and work in earnest".[2] This denunciation of "work-dodging", or "skiving", was to be echoed in many comments about public welfare services over the following centuries. By the twentieth century "welfarism" and the "welfare state" were used by some as terms of abuse, denoting a shameful abdication of individual responsibility in favour of weak-willed dependence on external assistance.

Others, however, put a different opinion. It was only common humanity, some felt, to provide relief for the needy and protection for the most disadvantaged sections of the community. John Donne, preaching at St Paul's, declared that the "duty of charity is a doctrine obvious to all". The moderate churchman, Edward Reynolds, declared that "God had given riches to us to do good with . . . for the good of our souls and the comfort of our poor brethren". A century later Dr Johnson declared that "a decent concern for the poor is the true test of civilization". And a century after that Disraeli denounced the restrictive Poor Law Act of 1834 as a disgrace to the country, declaring that it "announces to the world that in England poverty is a crime". Throughout the nineteenth century, and still more in the century that followed, there were many who proclaimed the need for more generous public provision to assist the more disadvantaged sections of the community.

When responsibility for welfare measures began to pass upwards to international bodies, exactly similar controversies arose there as had occurred within states. The politics of welfare ceased to be a purely national phenomenon. Just as some had declared that the provision of public assistance to individuals would undermine their sense of responsibility and sap their self-reliance, so now some held that *international* assistance would erode the responsibility of the individual state and sap its will to cope with its own difficulties. Under this view each state should provide for its own needs. It should seek by its own efforts to attain self-sustaining growth; and should by that means be enabled to create the services required to meet the needs of its own population, including the disadvantaged within them. The best way to bring this about would be to rely on the "market" to create the maximum freedom of economic interchange among states so that all could be equally independent. The relief of poverty in Bangladesh, under this view, was the responsibility of the Bangladeshi government alone; the care of refugees in Hong Kong was the responsibility of the Hong Kong (or the British) government only;

2. Quoted in Bruce, *The Coming of the Welfare State*, p. 47.

decisions on labour rights in Japan were questions solely for the Japanese government. No international body should interfere in such questions, whatever the scale of the problem faced. This was essentially an argument based on the supremacy of national sovereignty. Just as southerners in the United States had declared that each individual state should be able to decide for itself whether or not to abolish slavery, so now, it was held, national states should decide individually on all welfare questions which arose within their own borders; irrespective of any variations which might exist in the scale of the problems faced or in the resources available for meeting them.

But again many held a different view. These rejected the notion that the responsibilities of states or peoples ended suddenly at their own frontiers; and that each could therefore complacently turn their eyes away from the disadvantaged who lived on the other side of their borders. Just as, within states, it had come to be accepted that individual parishes could no longer be saddled with the responsibility of relieving local poverty, given the differences in the needs they faced and the resources they disposed of, making it necessary for national governments to take over the burden; so now, under this view, individual states, with their widely varying resources, could not be left to bear individually the burden of a national disaster, an influx of refugees, or an impoverished and disease-ridden urban shantytown, without assistance from elsewhere. No state was an island (whatever its geographical situation); and all must share in confronting problems which had become a common responsibility. Though the interests and resources of states might vary (and indeed precisely *because* of their differing needs and capabilities), they shared in an obligation to care for each other, and to join where necessary in common enterprises to protect their common interests.

There was another source of controversy (also mirroring corresponding disputes within states). One of the objections raised to the development of welfare services within states had always been the excessive costs these imposed on the public purse. It was because of the financial burden which their poor law responsibilities had entailed for the parishes that there were continual measures of "reform", such as that of 1834, designed to lessen the costs they bore. It was because of the ever-rising costs of national social services on national budgets in recent decades that conservative governments in developed states sought to introduce cuts in the level of services, and so the costs they entailed. The ever-rising cost of "welfare" was in such circles widely deplored. But there were others who believed that these services represented an essential means of remedying hardship and reducing inequalities. Far from being reduced, therefore, in a socially responsible society expenditure needed to be steadily *increased* to meet ever-growing needs. The expenditure to bring this about must therefore be found, even if it involved higher levels of taxation. And these was ample evidence that most people were willing to accept a higher burden of taxation for the sake of providing better health and social services.

This controversy too, with the globalization of politics, now arose at the international level equally. Here too there was scope for differences of view about the scale of the services to be provided by world bodies, and the cost that would therefore be placed on those who financed them. Some denounced the bureaucracy of the organizations providing the services, the corruption of the governments through which they operated, and the inefficiency of the services provided in this way. But they complained above all of the excessive burden such programmes placed on their own taxpayers: each state should decide individually how its money should be spent and should not have such choices taken on their behalf by distant do-gooders in world organizations. Their opponents pointed to the progressive nature of the system. For the rich states concerned, contributions represented only a tiny sum, yet they could provide substantial benefits for the recipients in poor countries. Some programmes fulfilled purposes that could not be undertaken by individual states but benfited all alike. Others provided assistance to the countries and individuals whose need was greatest. It was thus entirely justifiable that, for those purposes, some resources should be transferred out of the hands of richer states and used for programmes which were collectively decided. Such programmes could help to assure to all the right to freedom from hunger, freedom from fear, freedom from want and freedom from oppressive government: fundamental rights which the international community as a whole had a duty to safeguard.

A related controversy – also occurring at both levels – concerned the relative merits of private and public provision. One of the arguments directed against welfare services within states was that they necessitated the creation of a vast and expensive bureaucracy. This was too impersonal to be an understanding or effective dispenser of the services required. It created a vast empire for social workers, who acquired their own vested interest in a paternalistic system. The recipients of the services concerned were made vulnerable to the decisions of petty bureaucrats wielding huge powers, who did not always discharge their functions wisely or humanely. It was much better, under this view, to rely on private sources of assistance. On these grounds, in the nineteenth century in Britain and other countries private charity was often declared better than reliance on the interference of poor law administrators; while in more recent times many upheld "privatization", and recommended increasing reliance on private health care, private education, and private pensions, in place of those provided by collective agencies. Public provision should then be restricted to providing a safety net designed for the totally destitute alone.

Opponents pointed out that public services provided benefits for the recipient which no private agencies could match. Reliance on the limited and uncertain benevolence of private charity would not bring forward the resources required. Privatization of services would make them available only on the basis of price, so that they would be increasingly confined to those who could afford them. Those who were least well off, who were by definition those most in need of the services, would then be precisely those who were unable to make use of them. At the very least a divided society would be created, in which the privileged were able to procure superior private facilities, while the rest were obliged to rely on increasingly inadequate public services, continually deprived of the funds required to make them effective. What was needed, therefore, was not a lower but a higher level of public expenditure, financed from progressive taxation, so as to bring about a redistribution of welfare from those who were better off to those who were most disadvantaged.

An exactly similar political controversy surrounded the provision of global services. Here too some held that the level of provision should be strictly limited and confined to those recipients – in this case those states – which were most in need. International aid programmes should be restricted to the poorest states of all – the "least developed". They should be used for particular purposes only, and to promote self-help rather than to provide a feather-bed which deterred self-reliance. Assistance should be provided too by individual governments, acting bilaterally, rather than by a vast bureaucracy of international agencies, often under the political control of the recipient states themselves. Bilateral assistance would not only be more efficient. If sensitively managed, it should cause less dependence, since the recipient governments would be able to hold their own in dealing with a variety of separate donors, often acting in competition, than if they were made dependent on the decisions of single international agencies, such as the IMF and the World Bank. Even some services which served collective purposes, such as disaster relief, a world-wide weather watch or control of the traffic in narcotic drugs could better be provided through bilateral assistance to particular states than through large international agencies operating world-wide. If some transfer of resources was required, therefore, it could be better provided directly to the governments of developing countries by the donor states than through the wasteful intermediation of expensive and inefficient international organizations.

But, again, others held that private, that is bilateral, assistance could never be sufficient in scale to replace the funds made available through multilateral channels. Just as, within states, it was no longer feasible to rely on private charity alone to provide relief for the needy, as had been possible during the nineteenth century, so in the international system it was no longer possible to rely on the bilateral aid programmes which had been the principal source of external support to poor countries during the 1960s. Reliance on the wayward and limited donations of individual states would be far worse for the recipients than relying on the relatively reliable, impartial and non-political help afforded by international agencies. Still less was it possible to rely on individual countries becoming able, through rapid economic growth, to provide adequate services on an individual basis. If the provision of adequate care for refugees, satisfactory air navigation facilities, efficient anti-locust measures, or measures to prevent the spread of AIDS was to depend on individual national efforts alone, it would be many decades before some states were in a position to undertake those tasks effectively. Progress would need to be confined to the speed of the slowest (a rate of growth that would not be much speeded by bilateral assistance, since the very people who deplored international measures were the same who were opposed to generous bilateral aid programmes). If adequate services were to be provided, therefore, it could only be by means of common international services, financed on a progressive basis.

Global politics thus reproduced the debates of national political systems. Many of the conflicts that arose over the provision of international welfare services were similar to those which had been fought out for many years about national services. In both cases the controversies reflected a fundamental conflict of interests: between rich and poor, haves and have-nots. The rich had a double interest in resisting proposals to increase public provision for the disadvantaged. On the one hand they themselves were able to provide out of their own resources for their own needs: they were, by definition, not among the disadvantaged who most required the common services. On the other they contributed most (in absolute terms, though not necessarily proportionately) in tax contributions to the financing of services. It was for this reason that, in every age and in every century, it was the wealthy who resisted the extension of publicly provided services, and the poor who clamoured for their extension. It was the wealthier classes in eighteenth- and nineteenth-century Britain who protested at the burden on the rates represented by poor law provisions. It was the industrialists and traders in nineteenth-century Britain who complained of the tax burden, and restraints on their own freedom of action, which government legislation imposed. It was the Conservative party and those who supported it which in the following century complained at the cost of the national health service and old age pensions in Attlee's welfare state. And today it is the rich, in the US, Britain and other countries, who deplore the level of taxation imposed by the ever-rising costs of welfare services.

So too at the global level. There too it is the rich states which have been reluctant to finance services which mainly benefited the poor. There too it is the wealthy nations which have protested at the increasing budgets of the specialized agencies, and the burden that this imposed on each of them. And there too it is the poor who have called for expansion: the developing countries, which the common services most directly benefited, which have demanded higher budgets and a more adequate level of provision. So in global politics essentially similar problems – how much should be spent, in what way, on common services which would mainly benefit the disadvantaged – had led to political conflict of essentially similar kinds.

THE POLITICS OF GLOBAL WELFARE

The general principles involved in discussion of welfare questions in the international system are therefore not unlike those which arise within the national state.

What are the particular forms which the political conflict takes at the global level?

It is, in the first place, a struggle among groups of states. On each of the issues we have described – concerning the merits of self-reliance against public provision, concerning the burden of costs on the tax-payer, and concerning the relative merits of public and private services – there is a division of interest among different types of state. Just as, within states, those who represent the wealthier sections of the community will in general lay greater stress on self-reliance as against public provision, on the importance of reducing, or at least containing, the cost of services, and on the merits of private as against public provision, so in the global political system the wealthier states will in general favour the same alternatives: will stress the need for national self-reliance, for economy in the financing of international welfare programmes, and for private (that is bi-lateral) rather than for public (that is international) services; while the less well-off states will take the opposite view. Accordingly, it is scarcely surprising that the two camps are organized (like those who favour the two alternatives are into political parties within states) in appropriate organizations to promote their interests. These enable them to maximize their influence within the organizations where the battle occurs.

The poorer states of the world today combine to promote their common interests within the so-called Group of 77. This group seeks, within most of the specialized agencies as within the United Nations itself, to bring about a common voting position on each of the main questions which arise. They battle, on the one hand, for higher expenditure generally; and, on the other, for the *type* of expenditure which benefits more countries. The richer countries, correspondingly, have organized themselves to resist this pressure. They too meet to consult regularly: in the so-called "Geneva Group". This is a group of the chief developed countries which come together in regular meetings to discuss their general strategies towards the development of the UN system, and their tactics in confronting particular issues likely to emerge in the immediate future.

Both groups are concerned with one central question (over and above the more general issues of principle discussed above): how *much* should be spent on the services in question. Should the forthcoming budget – in the United Nations or each specialized agency – provide for a significant increase in real terms over the preceding period, or for a stand-still, or even for a decline? While, during the first thirty years after 1945, it was the Group of 77 which was mainly successful in this confrontation, leading to a steady and relatively rapid increase in the levels of spending in nearly all agencies, from the mid-seventies onwards that trend was reversed. From that point the richest countries, especially the two superpowers, began to exert very strong pressure for a reduction in the rate of increase and eventually brought something like a standstill in real growth. The unwillingness of the US in particular to accept significant increases, her withdrawal from one or two agencies, and her withholding of funds even in some bodies to which she did belong, had the effect that the overall level of spending in the system as a whole began to decline in real terms from 1980 onwards.

But the argument did not only concern the overall level of spending in the international system. Equally significant was the conflict concerning the *type* of spending. Within a national state this argument focused on the relative rate of increase in the budgets for education and defence, health and social security. That debate is undertaken not only in public discussions in parliament and the media. It occurs in private arguments between ministries; between ministers in the cabinet; and in an even more intensive argument between all spending ministries and ministers and the Treasury, or Ministry of Finance, seeking to check the overall rate of growth in spending.

In the global political system that struggle is more dispersed and disorganized. There is a series of quite separate skirmishes, rather than one decisive battle. Here there exists no body – such as the Treasury or the Cabinet – which exercises overall control of the expenditure undertaken. Each of the main spending departments – that is each agency – is to all intents and purposes totally independent. Though there have been endless attempts to bring about "coordination" (see Chapter 7 below), designed in part to establish priorities and so to bring about some correlation in levels of spending, it has had virtually no consequence. Each agency in practice reaches totally independent decisions on its future programmes. Thus the political battle takes place in a fragmented and decentralized way: in the attempt to influence the decisions reached, in the first place, by the Council of each agency, where the budget proposals are finalised, and in the second by their Assemblies where the budgets are finally endorsed or amended. Since the Assemblies have the final word, it might be thought that the battle which really counts is that which occurs within them. But in practice the most significant decisions are those on the *content* of the budgets reached within the Councils; and it is within them that usually the most significant political struggles occur. Because the agencies reach their decisions independently, there is no opportunity for any of the parties – that is any of the groups of governments – to discuss the most important decision of all: what should be the *relative* level of expenditure in each area: how much should be spent on international health measures (primarily by WHO) compared with the amount spent on educational programmes (primarily by UNESCO); how much is required for disaster relief, compared with the amount needed for the care of refugees (or even how much should go for the care of Arab refugees, undertaken by a separate organization, compared with the care of refugees generally); how much should be spent on the control of the international drugs traffic, compared with the amount spent on population programmes.

Nor is this the only difficulty in the way of reaching rational decisions on global social priorities. There is a further complication in the fact that some of the programmes are funded by the *voluntary* contributions of governments, while others come only from the official budgets of the agencies, to which all member states are bound to contribute. Moreover, some of the voluntary programmes, though financed through separate funds, are administered by the main specialized agencies concerned; while others have quite independent administrations. In addition some programmes among those administered by each agency are financed by the UN Development Programme: which is itself a voluntary fund, though it supports a wide range of activities.

This means that the administrative structure responsible for international social programmes is an immensely complex one. It is not a clearly ordered, carefully interrelated system, within which comparisons of expenditure can easily be undertaken and political choices made. It is rather a jungle of separate programmes and administrations, each operating independently, and each subject to its own complicated and convoluted internal political process (involving their chief officials as well as their governments).

The choice before individual governments is even more complicated. That choice is not simply one between different programmes serving different purposes – education against health, assistance for refugees against disaster relief, help for a programme against the drug traffic against help for a population programme, and so on. It is, in some cases at least, a choice between programmes that are publicly provided – that is undertaken by fully international bodies working in the field concerned – and those that are undertaken bilaterally, through the efforts of individual states, or groups of states (for example regional bodies), giving assistance to other states or groups of states. For some services, fortunately, this choice does not need to be made. There is only one body responsible for the notification of infectious diseases (WHO), or for the protection of labour standards (the ILO), or for the care of non-Arab refugees (the UN High Commission for Refugees); and there is no serious possibility of replacing these with bilateral arrangements. But in many cases the bilateral alternative is a real one. Assistance in the field of meteorology can be given bilaterally as well as through the World Meteorological Organization; help in the improvement of navigation aids can be given direct from government to government as well as through the International Civil Aviation organization. In other words an individual government, even though a part of the international system, and so a member of all the relevant international organizations, may decide to secure some of the objectives which that organization proclaims by alternative means: means which in effect compete with the publicly provided services. The choice between public and private services, so often a source of controversy within national states (for example in the field of education and health), thus emerges as a crucial one within the international political system too: in the form of a similar choice between private and public, bilateral or multilateral provision.

There is a further controversy, again comparable to one which arises within states: concerning the *scope* of the services – who they should aim to help. There are some internationally provided services which are indiscriminately available to all states (and therefore benefit individuals in all states). This is, for example, true of the meteorological services provided by the World Meteorological Organization, which are made available to all countries equally: they are intended to establish a fully international service, for example through the organization of weather stations and other sources of information benefiting all national services, and through research into general problems. But there are others which are deliberately intended to help the people of some states more than those of others. Thus a substantial part of the programme of most specialized agencies today goes for programmes of assistance specifically directed towards poorer countries: for example in agriculture (FAO), in education (UNESCO), in health facilities (WHO) and so on.

There are therefore in these cases two decisions to be reached. First, how much of the total budget should be spent on services available to all, and how much in the form of assistance for particular disadvantaged states. Secondly, if some is provided in the form of assistance, how should this be distributed? Should it go to *all* developing countries, or only to the forty or so "least developed" countries; all those which are experiencing a particular kind of difficulty, or all those who ask for help? Once more this problem is not unlike the question so often discussed concerning social services within states – whether provision should be universal or selective – or concerning the distribution of benefits among groups – between children and old people, or between the low-paid and the unemployed, for example. And that question is likely eventually to become an equally bitter source of political controversy within the global system.

Another controversy, which also mirrors comparable issues arising within states, concerns *how* international social services are provided. Within states there is concern about the bureaucratic nature of many social services organizations, their remoteness from the recipients, the difficulty of influencing their decisions, the reluctance in consequence of many of those in need to take up benefits to which they are entitled. At the global level similar problems arise. Bureaucracy is inevitably even greater in very large, cumbersome, multinational and multilingual bodies, without clear political direction, in which very substantial power lies in the hands of senior officials (see p. 179 below). As within states one of the obvious solutions, often proposed, is for greater decentralization than exists today: the diffusion of operations and management to local offices operating in the field, or at least in the capitals of each receiving country, so enabling more decisions to be taken at the local level. There is need, as within states, it is said, for much greater decision-making power to be entrusted to local officials and a greater flexibility in the way the decisions of the intergovernmental bodies are to be implemented. Bureaucratic infighting among the representatives of different organizations in each capital could be reduced it has been proposed, by according greater responsibility to the UN's resident representative in each capital so that they can impose a greater coherence on the operations of the system as a whole.[3]

Again there is room for obvious controversy (as within states once

3. This was first proposed twenty years ago in the Jackson Report on "the capacity of the UN system". Only small steps were taken to implement the report and many believe that much more needs to be done to integrate the dispersed efforts of different agencies within the UN system in individual capitals.

more) concerning the *structure* of each organization. How far is it representative of the international community generally? Should that be the most important consideration, or should the degree of representativeness be balanced by the needs of efficiency. These are, once more, issues not altogether unlike those which have arisen over centuries about national political institutions. What degree of "democracy" should be established, and how far should this be restricted in the interests of efficient government (as many more conservative politicians argued a century or so ago whenever demands for an extension of the franchise within states were proposed)? At first sight international bodies responsible for policy in this field – mainly the specialized agencies of the United Nations – are highly "democratic". All states are represented within them, and they operate on the principle of one-member-one-vote. This appearance is, however, misleading. Some are essentially oligarchic in their system of decision-making. The assemblies are often, in the specialized agencies even more than in the United Nations, not the most influential body. They usually meet at most once a year, and sometimes far less frequently: occasionally as rarely as every five years (as in the UPU). All the day-to-day work of each organization is thus undertaken by the Councils (sometimes known as the Governing Body, as in the ILO, or the Executive Committee, as in the WHO). This may meet as often as once a month, and never less than once a quarter; and, when it does meet, often for several days on end. It is here, therefore, that the most significant decisions are reached, including the vitally important recommendations on the forthcoming budget. In these bodies representation is often not "democratic", even in the usual UN sense. In many cases there is a higher level of representation for particular groups of states, almost always the most industrialized, and something like permanent membership for the largest of all. So, for example, it is provided in the constitution of the ILO that there should be special representation in the Governing Body for states of "chief industrial importance"; in the Council of the International Civil Aviation Organization for "states of major importance" in air transport; and in the International Maritime Organization for states with the largest interest in sea-borne trade and in international shipping services (which will inevitably mainly be developed countries). In the IMF and the World Bank votes (and therefore control) are distributed in proportion to financial contributions, which are themselves based on shares in world trade and world production: arrangements which give rich countries, only about 15 per cent of the membership, 60 per cent of the votes in both bodies. In all these cases, therefore, the constitutions of the agencies have ensured that the richer countries acquired a greater share of control than their numbers alone would warrant. Developing countries have made persistent efforts to secure increased representation in many of these bodies but have made little headway. The degree to which special representation of this kind should be provided for particular groups of states may therefore become an important source of controversy over future years.

Finally, a related issue concerns the way each organization is financed. This has considerable political significance, since it determines the degree to which the operations of each agency are redistributive in effect. Redistribution results partly, as we have seen, from the choice of programmes. But it depends also on the way in which contributions are assessed. If rich countries pay no more in proportion to their population than poor countries the only redistribution brought about would result from the way the money was spent (and many programmes benefit rich states as much as poor). Only in so far as the basis of contributions is progressive – as rich countries, that is, pay more proportionately than poor countries – will significant redistribution occur. The system of contributions is nearly always partially progressive, but the *degree* of progressiveness varies considerably: the proportion of the budget contributed by the US varies from 4·7 per cent (in the UPU) to 25 per cent (in WHO and the other large agencies). One of the forms which global politics may increasingly take is controversy concerning the system of redistribution established in each or all of these agencies.

In the global system of government, as in every other, therefore, differences of viewpoint have developed about the way in which the tasks performed are to be carried out. Differences concerning welfare services are bound to be especially acute, for they express fundamental differences of interest. How much should be spent, in what way, on what services who should be the main beneficiaries, and who the main contributors: these are not only important but deeply divisive questions, that cannot fail to stimulate strong differences of opinion. Because the international system of government remains at present relatively undeveloped, and is so far largely obscured from the public gaze, these conflicts are at present unpublicized and largely unconsidered by the general public. The sharp differences of interest and viewpoint which exist at the global level are often scarcely known and understood (in the way that corresponding conflicts concerning social services within the state are understood). As the international system of government develops, as the demands placed on it increase, and the needs to be confronted grow, those differences may begin to arouse political controversy as acute as that which surrounds similar problems within states.

The amounts that are spent on international services, and the variety of the benefits they provide, will undoubtedly grow. Within states the growth of welfare provision has matched the growth in national incomes so that the richer states become, the better the provision for the disadvantaged which is made. Even in the US, where the prevailing ethos is unfavourable to welfare spending, expenditure has steadily risen (even when conservative governments held power in Washington) and welfare spending is highest in those states, such as New York and California, where the standard of living is highest. So, in the international system too, rising standards of living are likely to provide a greater willingness to finance higher levels of social services expenditure. But the rate of increase will depend on the relative political influence of different types of nation, having different types of interest. Eventually, concern about the scale of disadvantage may, as within states, stimulate a more adequate global response. Expenditure on world social services may then becomes as important a feature of total international spending as is social services expenditure within states. A welfare world may increasingly be superimposed above the welfare state.

TRANSNATIONAL WELFARE PROBLEMS

Not all the issues which arise concerning international welfare services, however, are of the type we have been considering so far.

The controversies which we have been examining are those which arise between *governments* on those issues: conflicts of interest between rich and poor states, or between countries which are producers and consumers of the services concerned. These are therefore the problems of international rather than global politics: the politics which occur among different sovereign states of varying views and interests. They are relevant to the interests of individuals on these questions only in so far as the peoples of each state share common interests which will all be equally represented by the governments which rule them.

As we saw in Chapter 1, the assumption that the governments of states can effectively represent the varying views and interests of all their inhabitants is a misleading one. Those inhabitants have a wide range of views and interests, not always easily compatible. The views of some may be closer to the views of many inhabitants of other states, and the governments which represent them, than to the views put forward by their own governments. And some groups and individuals will have views that are different from those put forward by any government.

The first question that arises, therefore, is how far can any of the governments which represent states within an international organization represent the views even of their own peoples? This is not simply a question of whether they are "democratic". A government may have acquired power through free parliamentary elections, and won a majority of the votes in such elections (though even in democratic countries many governments hold power which have not won majority support), but may nonetheless fail to represent the views of that majority within the international organizations concerned. Few, if any, make any attempt to consult the views of their electorate on the questions which arise in such bodies. In practice they use the *general* authority they have acquired as the result of an election to do virtually what they please in this (as indeed almost any other) matter. They do not usually know whether their populations, still less particular sections of them, support larger or smaller programmes for each such body; nor if they prefer one programme to another. In practice they do exactly what they choose to do, on the basis of their own discretion. They are not even significantly influenced (as in some other areas of government) by knowledge of what their public opinion demands – or what the mass media assert public opinion demands. Most of the questions which arise are sufficiently esoteric, and the expenditure involved sufficiently marginal, for them to be ignored in normal political debate. The vast majority of the public know almost nothing about them. Only when the global political system acquires equal salience with national political systems, and the international public services equal prominence with national public services, will even "democratic" governments act on such questions in accordance with the views, known or believed, of their electorates.

But a large proportion of the governments which decide these questions are not even representative in this limited sense. Most governments which represent their states in international organizations do not even claim to exercise a mandate based on democratic elections. Even more than the "democratic" governments, therefore, they are able to decide for themselves what action they should take within the organizations: whether they should vote for more expenditure or less; more redistribution or less; more or less decentralization in administration; more or less selectivity in the distribution of benefits. Both the governments of poor countries, which receive the greatest net benefits from the services provided, and those of rich countries which make the largest net contributions (and often as a result have a major voice in the way they are spent) may therefore be unrepresentative, even in this crude sense, of the population of their countries.

But secondly, even if all the governments representing their countries were fully democratic, even if all had carefully ascertained the views of their populations on each question which arose, and even if all had conscientiously sought to reflect those views in the policies they followed, the way the services were run would not necessarily reflect the views of mankind generally. For the organization would still remain essentially representative of *governments*, presenting their own interpretation of the views of their populations. Opinions among the minorities in each population about such questions would still receive no expression in the deliberations of the controlling bodies. Yet those views, spread among a large number of countries, might be more widespread than that of many governments. In an increasingly integrated world society, in which many views of many kinds are held which are not reflected in the policies of governments, this situation may in time become increasingly unacceptable. There may increasingly emerge a demand for a political process which is *transnational* rather than international.

It may then no longer be accepted that the questions which arise concerning international welfare services – such as those discussed in this chapter – are questions for governments alone: to be argued about between governments in largely private debate, in the obscure committees and councils of specialized agencies, or in the memoranda exchanged between foreign offices and treasury departments within states. It will begin to be recognized that they are issues of some significance for the future distribution of wealth and welfare around the world. It will be seen that the decisions reached in these bodies may determine whether or not the disadvantaged among mankind, of various kinds, are to be assisted; whether labour standards are adequately protected; whether refugees will be adequately cared for; whether world diseases will be adequately checked; whether illiteracy will be significantly reduced; whether the trade in narcotic drugs will be sufficiently controlled; whether worthwhile measures to combat world-wide terrorism are undertaken; and so on. These are not small matters now. They are likely to become still less insignificant in the future. Many organizations and many individuals are therefore likely to seek a greater influence on the decisions which are reached about them than they are able to exercise today.

The first requirement, if this is to come about, is that there should be greater knowledge of the problems; of how they are being met today and what are the alternative courses of action available in the future. At present the activities of the agencies which operate in these various fields are wrapped in even greater obscurity than are the activities of the United Nations itself. Few regard them as important. Even those that do have little opportunity to find out what is being discussed in any of these bodies. Their deliberations receive virtually no coverage in the media (unless they are discussing personalities, such as the re-election of a Director-General especially unpopular with their own governments). Even if the tasks they perform are universally recognized as important and worthwhile, the decisions reached on the way these should be performed, the amount of money that should be spent on them, are reached behind closed doors, virtually unknown to the general public. Only when much more is known about those questions, and about the alternative courses of action available to the principal bodies concerned, will a greater degree of political awareness about their importance begin to emerge.

This should make it possible for a wider range of influences to make themselves felt on the actions of governments. But non-governmental views will only exercise a significant influence if channels are available through which they can be expressed. In theory a mechanism of this sort exists within the UN system. ECOSOC has recognized a role for a large number of non-governmental organizations, national and international, which are officially accredited, and accorded certain facilities within the system (see pp. 91–2 below). Opportunities are occasionally provided at which such bodies can make their opinions felt directly. But those who participate in such meetings are generally agreed that, as a means for affording effective influence on the decisions reached, they are largely without effect. They represent in practice a meaningless process of "consultation"; a formal nod to the existence of the voluntary agency lobby: providing an outlet for their energies and enthusiasm, allowing them possibly to feel important, but without representing any kind of commitment to heed their views. Those views remain at present virtually without influence on the decisions finally reached. They are probably rarely even known to the governmental representatives who reach the decisions. The system may be better than nothing at all. It represents at least a token recognition that views may be held on such questions by those who stand outside the charmed circle of governmental representatives. But it does not represent an alternative source of influence of any significance to that provided by governments.

Somewhat more effective (though how much more is questionable) are the "forums" or parallel conferences which nowadays usually take place at the same time as important intergovernmental conferences and seek to influence their outcome. Highly organized forums of this kind among non-governmental organizations took place, for example, at the time of the Stockholm conference on the environment in 1972, the Habitat conference on human habitation in 1976 and the main UN disarmament conferences. These (unlike the ECOSOC consultations) do win a considerable amount of publicity. They may therefore provide publicity for non-governmental views on the issues being discussed. They normally publish their own recommendations concerning the actions which the main conference should take: usually far more radical than the latter is likely to accept. And their proceedings are certainly known to the delegates to the main conferences and may even exercise some marginal influence on them. They are therefore a means by which non-governmental opinions can exert some influence, even if at present their effect is only marginal.

Over the years to come activity of this kind will certainly increase. Those who are actively concerned about the questions which arise in the social field – about the means of affording more effective protection of human rights, about the traffic in narcotics or the trade in unsafe pharmaceuticals, about the care of refugees or the relief of natural disasters, about the better protection of labour rights or the more effective supervision of safety standards in nuclear power generation – are likely to become better organized and better informed. They may become increasingly skilled in disseminating and publicizing their views and in exercising a direct influence on decision-taking bodies. And they will increasingly demand evidence that those bodies are beginning to take greater account of the views they express: views which, they will claim, are more representative of those of ordinary people than those that are put forward by governmental representatives.

As a result the political character of many of the issues which arise in these bodies, even when they are apparently purely technical or financial, will be increasingly recognized. The conflicting interests of various sections of the population in different countries in the adoption of different policies and courses of action will become more visible and, as a result, the conflicts which occur over such questions will become as significant within the political consciousness of ordinary citizens as those which occur over the welfare services provided within their own states. Their political actions may then be directed as much to influencing global decisions on those questions as they are to influencing comparable decisions within the national state.

4 The Protection of the Environment

THE INTERNATIONALIZATION OF THE ENVIRONMENT

But citizens have found that there are other tasks, of increasing concern to them, which national governments are no longer capable of performing. They are conscious of the threat which industrialization within their own states poses to the national environment. They are concerned about the increasingly serious pollution of air and water resulting from factory emissions and the dumping of industrial waste produced by rapid economic growth. They are anxious about the threats to soil and climate which over-intensive systems of agriculture have brought about. They are increasingly aware of the impact of urbanization, hastened by excessive population increase, on the quality of life which they and, even more, their children can enjoy. They are anxious about the green-house effect and long-term climatic change. They are concerned about the depletion of the world's natural resources which has already resulted from economic development in industrialized countries, and will be hugely increased as a result of the spread of that process to other parts of the world. They are worried at the destruction or despoiling of their natural habitats. They already demand, with increasing intensity, action by national governments to meet these concerns. But they are increasingly conscious that many of these problems cannot be overcome by the action of individual states alone.

National governments themselves have only relatively recently, and then haltingly, become aware of these problems. For long they were content that individuals should seek their own livelihoods in their own way, unrestrained by the interference of central authorities, believing that the impact which these activities might have on the quality of life of their population generally was too marginal to require any restraining action. They thus until recently allowed any new technology likely to maximize production to be freely developed, and permitted the necessary factories to be constructed, cheek by jowl with residential accommodation, wherever enterprising industrialists might think fit. Beyond providing (eventually) elementary sanitation to reduce the worst risk to health of overcrowded cities, little attempt was made to interfere with the free course of industrial and commercial enterprise. Only in a few areas did there begin to be some concern that unrestrained industrialization might bring long-term costs and growing threats to resources. In the United States from the end of the nineteenth century an influential conservation movement preached the need for reforestation and the conservation of threatened natural resources; and received for a time powerful support from President Theodore Roosevelt. That view, however, was not widely heeded. For long it did not affect the prevailing belief that governments should not interfere to restrain the natural exuberance of uninhibited economic activity.

Only slowly, during the course of the last fifty or sixty years, did governments begin to become more willing to accept responsibility for protecting the quality of life of their citizens and the environment which they inhabited. They started, through planning regulations, to protect residential areas from the blight and disturbance of industrial development, and so to limit marginally the adverse effect of industrial pollution. They became more aware of the threat, at least to national if not to personal interests, from the rapid depletion of natural resources: so a whole series of high-powered commissions were appointed by US presidents to advise on the steps which should be taken to meet that danger. They began to take steps to restrict activities which caused the most serious pollution of air and water.

In many cases they were awakened by particular environmental disasters, and the public concern they aroused, to dangers which had previously been ignored. The dustbowls of Arizona and Oklahoma stimulated new efforts to encourage agricultural practices less likely to result in the erosion of valuable agricultural soil. The disastrous smog of 1953 in Britain, causing 3,000 deaths within a month, led a British government to introduce the 1956 Clean Air Act, which had a dramatic effect in reducing water and air pollution in Britain and was widely followed by similar measures elsewhere. The destructive effect of chemical pesticides on US wild life, and the publicity given to this by Rachel Carson's book *Silent Spring*, convinced US Federal and state governments to introduce more rigorous regulation of the use of agricultural chemicals; action which again was followed by similar steps elsewhere. Disastrous oil spills, for example the Torrey Canyon disaster off the British coast in 1957, and the equally serious spillage off Santa Barbara in California the following year, caused both governments to tighten regulations governing the operation of oil tankers off their coasts. The ever-rising noise of jet aircraft, and the protests this aroused from those living near airports, caused governments to restrict the landing of aircraft at night, and in some cases to impose other restrictions to reduce noise levels.

Action on these lines was increasingly demanded by a growing range of environmental groups in most developed countries. These ranged in style from the practical, sober and scientific to the strident, militant and semi-political. In time they began to have an increasing influence, both on the general public, and, as a result, on governments. Their concern at first was with the national environment and national legislation to protect it. But it quickly began to become clear to those groups, to the publics they appealed to, and to national governments, that many of the worst problems that were faced were not such as national governments were capable of dealing with individually. The problems that were being confronted were in many cases not national but international, and they could be effectively confronted not by national but only by international action.

The problem of the depletion of natural resources, for example, which US national commissions had looked at in such detail, was (as those commissions themselves recognized) not one that any government could deal with in isolation. Even the United States, far more self-sufficient in resources than most countries, relied for some essential minerals – for example manganese, chrome, cobalt and, increasingly, oil – on imported supplies; and it was only international, not national, action that could safeguard these. Most other states, apart from the Soviet Union, which was equally fortunate, were far more obviously dependent on mineral and other resources imported from elsewhere. If there was a danger of depletion, therefore, it was a danger which affected all countries equally. And if effective measures were to be taken to reduce that risk, only international measures would be sufficient. That is why, from the early seventies, the so-called Club of Rome and other bodies began to call, sometimes in excessively alarmist tones, for more effective international management and husbanding of declining world resources if disaster was to be averted.

Pollution of the sea was equally obviously a problem no individual government could deal with effectively. However rigorous the regulations each might promulgate concerning, for example, the construction, loading, manning and navigation of its own oil-tankers and other ships, these could not safeguard its coasts if the ships of other states were not similarly regulated. Because of their recognition of a common interest in the use of the seas which all used, maritime states had already, before the First World War, begun to discuss the establishment of international standards in the field of safety at sea. An international convention on that question was first prepared at that time (following the *Titanic* disaster) and, in revised form, came into effect in 1929; to be replaced in 1948, by another which has since been regularly revised. Marine pollution, which could affect all coastal states and all individuals using the oceans, equally clearly needed to be dealt with on an international basis. It was first considered in a committee of the League of Nations in 1934–5. An international convention laying down the measures signatories would take to reduce pollution was signed in 1954, and has been gradually extended and strengthened since. Subsequent conventions have given greater powers to coastal states in dealing with such disasters and in securing adequate compensation for them. A Marine Environment Protection Committee, established by the International Maritime Organization, has supervised the application of these measures and seeks to safeguard the marine environment generally. Standards relating to the training of crews, the construction of ships, the storage within them of oil and other dangerous cargoes, have been laid down. In this way an attempt has been made to provide for marine pollution the type of international regulation so obviously required.

Individual states were equally unable to cope adequately with pollution of the air. Here too the actions taken by one state would not necessarily be sufficient to protect it from threats which emanated from another. However vigorous the regulations concerning the emission from power stations in Sweden or Canada, these could not safeguard the inhabitants of those countries from acid rain originating in Britain or the United States. The same applies, equally self-evidently, to protection from nuclear radiation: however efficient the safety standards applied for the construction of nuclear reactors in Western Europe, these could not save their populations from the effect of accidents to power stations constructed in other countries, such as the Soviet Union. In other cases, even if there was no direct cross-border effect international action might still be required to coordinate the action necessary in a number of states. For example, no individual country could effectively protect itself from the effects of car exhaust emissions in destroying forests or polluting cities, unless they were matched by similar action taken in other countries: for if every country imposed its own regulations independently, manufacturers would be obliged to try to meet a wide range of differing pollution standards for each of the cars they manufactured, which was obviously impractical. If action was to be taken on the question at all, therefore, it must obviously be done on an international basis. And if individuals and groups were concerned on the question, it was international decisions which needed to be influenced.

The same thing applied to regulation of the use of agricultural pesticides and other chemicals. It was no use particular countries imposing restrictions on their use within their own borders (as developed countries, in response to powerful public pressures, increasingly did) if their companies continued to sell them to less advanced countries which had not formulated the necessary legislation. Not only would this mean that the same environmental damage which the governments concerned were seeking to prevent within their own borders would continue in other parts of the world. They would not even protect their own populations, since food produced within the foreign countries concerned would be reimported and consumed within their own territory. Only regulation that was world-wide in its effect could protect the interests of individuals in all countries. And it was world-wide action which was therefore required to meet the concern of environmentalists everywhere.

The safeguarding of energy supplies too was no longer a question which could be left to individual states. Continued depletion of resources in individual countries would eventually have consequences for the world as a whole. The wasteful use of energy, and of the fossil fuels which provided it, in a few rich countries, could mean that developing nations would find supplies restricted when they themselves were in a position to use equivalent amounts, or at least would have to pay far more to acquire them. It was in recognition of the common interest of all states in the preservation of the earth's precious natural minerals that the United Nations set up its Committee on Natural Resources to maintain a continuing watch on the supply and use of mineral and other resources in 1970. The destruction of some resources, even though they were undeniably the product of the country which possessed them, could have consequences that were global. Nobody disputed that the forests existing in the territory of one state belonged to that country and no other. But the destruction of those forests through excessive commercial exploitation, or even for firewood, would eventually affect many who lived in other countries as well. If the government of Brazil failed to prevent the destruction of its Amazonian jungle, there could be consequences for climatic conditions all over the world. In that sense each government was in the position of guardian or trustee for the international community as a whole. And every member of that community thus had a legitimate interest in scrutinizing the way that responsibility was fulfilled elsewhere.

International action was sometimes necessary for another reason. There were some areas of the world which did not clearly belong to any state, yet had an important environmental significance. Antarctica, for example, represented a unique environment which was especially vulnerable to serious, and possibly permanent, damage if wrongly used and so manifestly required to be protected. It was known to contain valuable resources – above all deposits of oil and gas – which some countries were increasingly anxious to exploit, especially in the off-shore areas. Yet no individual government had either the right or the power to undertake the necessary regulation to prevent serious damage. Here, self-evidently, some form of international regulation – more genuinely international, that is, than could be provided by the self-appointed, self-selected parties to the Antarctic Treaty – needed to be established if an effective and internationally acceptable system of control was to be provided. A similar situation existed in the two-thirds of the world's surface covered by the oceans. Here too new forms of exploitation – not only off-shore oil and gas production, but large-scale mechanized fishing and, in the not too distant future, the mining of mineral resources from the sea-bed itself – threatened environmental damage which no individual government was able to prevent. Here too, self-evidently, only international action could provide the type of regulation that was necessary. It was on these grounds that the regulation to be provided in these areas, beyond the limits of national jurisdiction, was increasingly discussed in a number of international bodies: in international fisheries commissions and the International Whaling Commission, above all at the Conference on the Law of the Sea, where a new set of legal rules on these questions was drawn up. Another such region was Outer Space, where again no states claimed sovereignty, but which were equally vulnerable to serious damage from a number of human activities. Threats to make use of the area for military purposes (for example in President Reagan's Star Wars proposal), the increasing use of aerosols widely believed to be damaging to the biosphere through the reduction of ozone, scientific experiments (such as one, undertaken in the US which involved sending copper needles into space, and was believed by some to threatened permanently damaging consequences) could have serious and possible irreparable effects if there existed no system by which they could be regulated. In all such non-national areas, therefore, the need for some system of global monitoring and control was especially manifest.

Nowhere was the need for world-wide action more apparent than to secure the preservation of plant and animal species increasingly threatened by the encroachment of human activities on their traditional habitats. Vast numbers of species had already been lost for ever and countless others were being extinguished every year. Many more would disappear unless urgent action was taken to preserve them. Some cooperation had been established among non-governmental bodies for this purpose from early in the century. An international convention for the "protection of birds useful to agriculture", in danger of being destroyed by hunting and other activities, was signed in 1902. A bilateral treaty on the protection of migratory birds was signed between the US and Canada in 1916, and subsequently joined by a number of other governments. A Convention on the Preservation of Fauna and Flora in their Natural States was signed in London in 1933, and was followed by a Convention on Nature Protection and Wildlife Preservation in the Western Hemisphere in 1937. A number of unofficial bodies began to be set up with an interest in this subject. An International Committee for Bird Preservation was established in London in 1922. In 1934 an International Office for the Protection of Nature was established in Brussels, though it was at that stage little more than a documentation centre. More formal steps were taken after the Second World War. The International Union for the Protection of Nature was set up in 1948, later becoming the International Union for the Conservation of Nature and Natural Resources (ICUN), the principal non-governmental organization active in this field. Scientific and semi-official bodies of this kind began to be supported by campaigning organizations, concerned particularly with alerting public opinion to the problem: such as the World Wildlife Fund and many similar organizations. International legislation began to cover a wider range of species: for example, in the Endangered Species Convention, under which governments pledged themselves to ban the import of products made from animal species threatened with extinction. At the same time new efforts were made, both privately and publicly, to preserve the seeds of threatened plant species.

In each of these areas, therefore, it had become apparent that the natural environment, about which so many people had begun to become concerned, could be protected only by international action. That environment belonged to the world as a whole. It was not conveniently parcelled out into convenient national compartments, each of them the property and responsibility of 160 different governments. It was an integrated whole, an undivided continium, a seamless web. Effective action to protect it from the dangers which increasingly threatened it, it was now understood, could only be taken at a world-wide level.

THE POLITICS OF THE ENVIRONMENT

To outward appearances the desire to protect the environment from the forces which might do it harm is an uncontroversial one. Everybody loves the natural world. All would like to see it preserved from damage. It might therefore be thought that efforts to achieve that end would arouse little political controversy.

But the fact that ultimate objectives are generally desired does not prevent substantial disagreement about the means of achieving them. Those differences can concern (among other things) the *extent* to which the objective can reasonably be attained; the relative importance to be accorded to rival and competing aims; the specific measures which are proposed for attaining even those objectives which are accepted; and the distribution of the costs of attaining them.

Conflict on all of these points has emerged in relation to the protection of the environment. Thus many who supported the general objective of preserving the environment from unacceptable harm disagreed on the amount of damage which was acceptable and the price which could reasonably be paid for the sake of preventing it. Secondly, many who saw the protection of the environment as a desirable objective believed that there were other aims, for example the achievement of a reasonable standard of living for their people, which had to be balanced against that objective. Thirdly, even if it was agreed, in a general way, that a particular form of environmental damage – say acid rain – should be reduced, there could still be disagreement on the appropriateness of a particular solution that was proposed – such as highly expensive modifications to power stations at substantial cost to the electricity consumer. Finally, even if all these propositions were accepted, there could still be disagreement about how the measures agreed to be necessary should be undertaken and how they should be financed.

All these questions were the subject of acrimonious political controversy within states. The importance to be accorded to protecting the environment in relation to other desirable aims was discussed at length: above all in controversy about the relative value to be placed on continued economic growth on the one hand and environmental protection on the other. The most ardent campaigners for firm action to preserve the environment were willing to pay a substantial price to achieve that end; in some cases prepared to forego economic development altogether if that was necessary to secure a better quality of life and a lessened depletion of threatened natural resources, demanding in its place a "steady state economy". Others held that, however desirable it might be to achieve environmental objectives, these could not override altogether the aim of securing further improvements in living standards, especially for less privileged members of society; and that the former aim must always therefore be carefully balanced against the latter.

Differences on this point reflected to some extent (or were said to reflect) a difference in interests among different sections of a population. Concern for the environment, it was pointed out, is felt most strongly among relatively well-off people who, no longer requiring themselves to worry too much about where their next meal was coming from, could afford to devote their attentions instead to less immediate problems: the threat to endangered species, the need for cleaner air and water, and the noxious effects of car exhausts. The mass of less privileged people, living close to the margins of existence, were said to attach greater importance to securing improvements in their modest standards of living, and were not necessarily willing to sacrifice such improvements for the sake of benefits which appeared to them relatively marginal. It is doubtful if either rich or poor necessarily saw their interests in the relatively crude way these descriptions suggested. It might be truer to say that contrasting opinions concerning the environment reflected differences in the values of individuals: in particular the relative valuation placed on higher material benefits, resulting from higher rates of production, and on intangible, immaterial benefits, resulting from higher environmental quality. But it is probably the case that, on average, concern about the latter was more widespread and more powerful among relatively prosperous middle-class sections of the population and those who represented their views politically; while a higher importance was attached to rising standards of living among the less well-off and the political parties which represented their opinions.

But these contrasting attitudes reflected a more fundamental division: not simply between those who attached more importance to material growth and those who attached more to quality of life, still less that between the better off and the less well off. It was also a conflict about the relative importance of short-term and long-term benefits. The manufacturer who protested against the efforts of pressure groups, parliaments and public authorities to impose environmental controls which would raise his costs of production, was concerned with *immediate* costs, those directly related to the manufacture of the goods in question; and he would argue that the reduction of those costs was desirable not only in his own interest, because it maximized the sales and profits, but in those of the consumer and so of society generally, because it brought about the production of goods that were in demand more cheaply than would otherwise be the case. Those who favoured environmental controls on the other hand, believed that the cheapness of production brought about under traditional calculations was an illusion which ignored the "external" costs, that is, those imposed on the community as a whole by the use of those methods. The environmental damage caused by them, whether it was the pollution of rivers, atmosphere and soil, noise pollution, the exhaustion of resources, damage to the climate or the biosphere, or a threat to surviving natural species, would have to be paid for eventually. Rivers, atmosphere and soil would ultimately need to be cleaned or rehabilitated; those whose health had been damaged would need to receive medical treatment (or their lives would be shortened, another cost); slag-heaps and spoils would need to be cleared; forests would need to be replanted. All these things cost money. Thus the real, long-term cost of the industrial practices concerned was much greater than were the apparent short-term costs. If this, the cost to the community as a whole, was taken into account, the products were not so cheaply produced as appeared at first sight. And it was economically justifiable to demand that protective action should be taken, if necessary at the cost of the industrialist himself, on the principle that the polluter should pay; or even to ban the practices concerned altogether.

But there was another, and still wider, issue which these questions raised: the conflict between the freedom of the individual – whether the manufacturer of chemicals resisting the imposition of environmental controls, the commercial whaler refusing to submit to limits on his catch, or the parent wishing to produce as large a family as possible – and that of the community as a whole, demanding to restrict those rights in the common interest. For the chemical manufacturer the issue was not between a short-term and a long-term gain: even over the long-term he personally might benefit if no environmental controls were imposed, since he might live in a salubrious rural area far from his factory, and believe that it was far more important that his products should sell at a reasonable price (and that he should make a substantial profit) than that rivers in the immediate vicinity of his factory should be marginally cleaner than before. In his view, therefore, the important wider objective was that the freedom of commercial enterprise should be interfered with as little as possible. The Norwegian whaler might believe that it was far more important, for the sake of the consumer as well as himself, that, if he was willing to undergo substantial danger for the sake of securing an additional supply of valuable protein, he should be allowed to do so without restraint from an authority which he might not recognize, than that a larger number of whales were enabled to survive. The parents wishing to add yet another child to an already extensive family might believe that it was far more important that they should have the freedom to choose for themselves about such questions than that the future population of the world should be marginally reduced. Against this, in all these cases, public authorities, believing themselves responsible for looking after the interests of the community generally – the interests of the future as well as the present – might feel justified in promoting what they saw as the wider public interest at the expense of the narrow private interests of individual. So, in many cases, controversies on environmental issues were concerned not merely with the type of action required to protect the environment, but with the degree to which individual liberties might be restricted for that purpose: the balance between regulation and "deregulation".

The choices involved in such cases are not necessarily simple either-or propositions. On each of these questions – the choice to be made between growth or quality of life, those who already have the material well-being they want and those who require more, short-term and long-term advantage and private freedom or public benefit – many may take a view somewhere in the middle. They will favour some growth and some environmental protection, some consideration of the strongly held views of those who already have enough, and some of the views of those who believe they need more, a balance between short-term advantage and long-term cost, between the private right of freedom of enterprise and the public right of restraint for the general good. But the fact that the middle view is possible, and even widespread, does not mean that the choices are not real ones. The choice still has to be made; and the *relative* importance attached to each alternative becomes, therefore, in domestic political systems, an issue of key importance. With the declining significance of traditional subjects of political controversy – concerning the distribution of power and wealth within society – such issues have indeed become today (as the rising popularity and influence of "green parties" and ecological movements demonstrate) among the most vital and bitterly disputed political issues of the day.

THE GLOBAL POLITICS OF THE ENVIRONMENT

Each of the political choices we have described also occurs in the global political system.

Here too, conflict arises between those who believe that nothing can be more important than attaining the highest possible rate of growth, and those who attach a greater value to the protection of the global environment. And here too it is a difference of view especially between richer and poorer: in this case richer and poorer states. While the former do not discount the importance of avoiding excessive depletion of scarce resources and preventing damage to the world's natural ecology, they believe that both aims can be reconciled with that of securing steady economic growth including the industrialization of many nations at present relatively undeveloped. Even developed states, they suggest, still face the problem of poverty among significant sections of their populations, as well as a general desire for a continued rise in living standards: they too must therefore maintain their efforts to bring about economic growth and ever-rising standards of living. Less developed countries, facing far worse problems, including widespread destitution among the majority of their populations, can still less be expected to forego economic development for the sake of the relatively marginal benefits of reduced pollution and other environmental hazards.

Such attitudes are seen by their opponents as narrow and short-sighted. All mankind, they assert, has a paramount interest in husbanding the resources, and preserving the environment, of an overcrowded planet. All must therefore learn, whatever their existing condition, to adjust their aspirations and their policies to that uncomfortable fact. Unless they restrain their appetite for growth, or at the very minimum acquire a new conception of the type and speed of growth that is desirable, all will be condemned to disaster. Only the adoption of totally new goals – such as environmentally aware, resource-conscious, "self-sustaining" growth, of a type that might be maintained without risk to environment or resources – will avert that threat which unrestrained growth at present poses to an endangered planet.

This controversy, like that which occurs within states, matches the conflicting interests of different groups within international society. Here too the less well off are not always convinced of the relevance to their own situation of the arguments which more privileged sections of that community thrust at them. Countries as yet to be industrialized, and so with no experience of industrial pollution, are not always apprehensive of the dangers which that process might bring. Conscious of little except their own poverty, and believing that nothing is more important for their populations than escape from that condition, they do not always appreciate being told that they should be enlightened and far-sighted: that they should devote themselves to agricultural rather than industrial development, to "intermediate" or "appropriate" rather than advanced technology, handicrafts and spinning-wheels rather than steel mills and chemical plants. Pollution is in their view a problem the rich have created for themselves which they should solve in whatever way they please. It is not a problem which they themselves yet face; and even when they do, they tend to believe, if it is the price that has to be paid for the sake of securing a higher standard of living for their people, it is probably a price worth paying. Such states therefore, in the international discussions which increasingly took place from the mid-60s onward, tended to decry excessive emphasis on restricting economic growth, the "steady state" economy and the "limits to growth". They were unwilling to be deterred, by awful warnings of the disasters which might ultimately confront them, from the same course of industrial development which the rich countries themselves had, in their own day, so wholeheartedly embraced.

The rich countries had a different interest. Maximizing rates of growth was no longer the only important aim for them. The fact that they themselves had created some of the problems confronting the world environment through their own industrialization programmes did not deter them from deploring a similar course of action by others, threatening a global environment which they increasingly saw as common to all. If different methods of agriculture were required to reduce erosion and desertification, if new types of forestry were needed to prevent the exhaustion of the jungles, if new types of industrialization were desirable, relying on manpower rather than resources, they had no hesitation in advocating them to other countries which might not yet have learnt those lessons. If it was increasingly necessary that aid programmes should take careful account of the environmental consequences of each project, they did not refrain from proposing such changes. Their interests as environmental consumers gave them, in their own eyes, the right to demand, for example in the development programmes assisted by the World Bank, whose operations they still controlled, systems of production which would not damage that interest. So, increasingly, they felt fully entitled to pass judgement on the production methods adopted by other countries which saw their interests in different terms (even if they closely resembled those which they themselves had adopted in earlier times). In the international system too the conflict was often at root one between short-term and long-term interests: the immediate costs of conforming with regulatory standards, even if this involved some reduction in production efficiency over the short-term against the eventual cost of progressive environmental degradation over the long-term. The environmentally-conscious states which called for stricter environmental standards to be maintained by all states, and for environmental consideration to be taken into account in all aid programmes, declared themselves to be protecting the long-term interests of mankind in preserving an endangered planet against the short-term benefits of immediate gains in industrial production. Cutting down the forests of Brazil or Nepal might bring immediate gains both to the foresters themselves and to their governments; but only at huge cost to the peoples of other countries and the world as a whole, and even to their own people in the long-term. The extension of grazing areas in the south of the Sahara might bring immediate benefits to the pastoral people of the area themselves; but only at vast cost – in eventual desertification – to the peoples of the entire region over the long-term. Governments were responsible, they maintained, not only for the welfare of their present population but for that of their children and many generations yet unborn. It was thus worth sacrificing some economic development over the short-term for the sake of ensuring a better future for the world as a whole over the long term.

Those governments, rich and poor, which resisted such pleas were unwilling to turn their eyes so far towards the unknown dangers of an unknown future. They were more conscious of the needs of the moment: in the form of mouths inadequately fed and backs inadequately clothed, families unhoused and schools unbuilt. While they did not deny the need to look ahead, to take some account of the possible long-term costs of development, these were not seen as sufficiently threatening in the immediate to deter them – especially states whose populations were manifestly deprived of many basic essentials – from proceeding with their ambitious plans for economic development. The known needs of the present, they believed, could not be altogether subordinated to the unknown requirements of the future.

Finally here too, in the international as in the domestic political system, the conflict was ultimately one between social and individual purposes: how far could the fundamental right of each state to decide its own policies independently legitimately be restrained for the sake of safeguarding the interests of other states, or of the international community as a whole? There were some states, both rich and poor, which claimed that, whatever the alleged environmental damage resulting from particular processes or activities, they must remain free to undertake them if they were determined to do so in their own economic interests. They remained sovereign states, having the right to pursue their own interests in the way they thought best; and there was no international law, still less any effective international authority, which could prevent them from doing so. So however vociferously other states and unofficial groups might complain, and whatever the rulings of the International Whaling Council, states which believed that whaling activities were vitally important economic enterprises – such as Japan, Norway and Iceland – insisted that they would continue to go their own way in order to protect those interests. However urgently the institutions of the EEC or individual governments of the Community might demand that Britain should abandon the dumping of nuclear waste in the Irish sea or sewage sludge in the North Sea, its government continued to insist that it alone must be the final judge of what level of dumping was acceptable. However insistently Germany and the Netherlands might demand tighter controls on the dumping of industrial wastes in the Rhine, the Swiss government might continue to maintain that it alone could determine, in the light of its economic interests, how far it would comply.

Here was the central issue surrounding environmental politics (and indeed international politics generally) in the modern world. Some of the most important political disputes now concerned environmental questions: what type of standard or restriction was necessary for what purposes and how rigorously should they be applied in particular cases? It led to continual conflict, which divided rich countries from each other as often as rich countries from poor. But it concerned above all the traditional claim of sovereignty. Over and over again some states would resist a call for higher standards – to reduce acid rain or emission from car exhausts or the use of pesticides; while others, usually those on the receiving end – Sweden, Canada and a number of developing countries – called equally insistently for higher standards and more effective compliance.

Thus environmental issues began to occupy an important position in international politics generally. Conflicting interests and attitudes were reflected in the conflicting decisions taken by different states within the main international bodies concerned with the question. It was in those bodies that, in theory, such disputes should have been resolved. But though they were fought over with considerable intensity, they could not always be finally decided there.

This was partly because there was no clear-cut division of responsibility among international organizations, and so no final authority on the question. The only intergovernmental body specifically concerned with environmental matters is the United Nations Environment Programme. This was set up as a consequence of the Stockholm Conference on the international environment of 1972, with the function of organizing work in this field within the UN system. It was established with its headquarters in Nairobi. It was to establish a global environmental monitoring system to record information about the world environment, obtained mainly from national and regional bodies and from the specialized agencies, and undertake other international tasks relating to the world environment. It has launched the Earthwatch monitoring system; established programmes on desertification and soil erosion; undertaken studies and programmes relating to the marine environment, including a successful scheme for the reduction of pollution in the Mediterranean; and coordinated a number of programmes run mainly by the specialized agencies: for example, the WHO's programme of atmospheric pollution, the World Meteorological Organization's programme to study the composition of the atmosphere, the Intergovernmental Global Ocean Station System (IGOSS), run by WMO and the International Oceanographical Commission, for measuring marine pollution, and the Global Investigation of Pollution in the Marine Environment, under the IOC.

However, UNEP has no exclusive jurisdiction in this area. It does not even exercise overall control of all environmental activities within the UN system. The family of UN agencies is not (as we shall see in Chapter 7) a tidy and well-structured system, in which a single body has ultimate authority for a specific area of activity. It is an assemblage of virtually independent agencies, linked, in only the most tenuous way, within the UN "family". There is no clear line of command, and only haphazard and usually ineffective "coordination" by a number of different bodies (pp. 156ff. below). Each of the specialized agencies attaches great importance to maintaining its "autonomy" and to maintaining its own programme in areas in which it was interested. A number of them had a legitimate interest in particular aspects of the world environment even before UNEP was established and had embarked on various activities relating to these. They were not willing to relinquish these responsibilities nor even to accept any significant degree of coordination by UNEP or any other external body. Some tasks within this area were undertaken by regional bodies, such as the EEC (altogether outside the UN system); by the regional economic commissions (such as the Economic Commission for Europe and the Economic Commission for Latin America); or by specialized *ad hoc* bodies (for example, the intergovernmental body set up to deal with pollution in the North Sea, which was not, like that established to deal with the Mediterranean, set up under the auspices of UNEP). In other words there was a jungle of different organizations, each having an interest in particular aspects of the problem and each operating largely independently of the others.

But not only was responsibility for environmental questions dispersed. Funding was totally inadequate. UNEP could only have acquired a leading role within this system, with a clear and well-recognized authority over the activities of other agencies, if it disposed of substantial and reliable sources of finance, enabling it to become the piper which called the tune. In fact, its funding came only from voluntary donations, mainly from a handful of countries (in the mid-eighties 75 per cent of the budget was provided by half-a-dozen countries). This budget was from the beginning quite inadequate even to cover its own tasks, let alone to fund any performed by other agencies. Nor was the UN Development Programme (UNDP), though it financed some projects in this field, able to undertake any significant degree of coordination, if only because this was only a relatively minor area of its activity, in which it claimed no special expertise. The World Bank finances a number of projects which have substantial implications for the environment, but it too makes no claim to any general coordinating role.

This has prevented the UN system in general, and UNEP in particular, from acting, as many had hoped, as the principal focus for activity in this area and the recognized instrument for protecting the international environment. Even the monitoring task, which many saw as UNEP's most important function, has not been adequately performed because of the lack of resources and the division of responsibilities. Other tasks have been even less adequately undertaken. Though substantial efforts have been devoted to a programme to combat desertification in the Western Sahara, this has achieved little, because of the large number of separate agencies involved and the minimal resources available for the purpose. International bodies have not been able to prevent large scale deforestation – especially in Latin America and South East Asia – doing little but utter occasional deploring noises, because no adequate funds have been available to assist diversification or promote replanting. Development assistance has continued to be given to programmes, especially large-scale hydro-electric schemes, which have had disastrous environmental effects. The earth's biosphere continues to be threatened by the failure to control adequately the use of aerosols and car emissions. Acid rain continues to pollute lakes, rivers and forests. The division of authority within the system, and the tiny budget available to UNEP (two facts which are closely related), have left them hopelessly ill-equipped to play the leading role in combating these threats.

The central political issues were therefore: how much effort should be devoted to the task of protecting the international environment; what resources were required for doing this; and how should those resources be allocated? There was a wide range of opinions and attitudes on those questions. The differences which existed did not, like most other international issues, reflect any clear-cut political division of opinion. They were not straightforward differences between rich states and poor, still less between communist and non-communist, democratic and authoritarian, European and North American against Asian and Latin American states. The division was primarily between those states which attached prime importance to industrial growth at almost any cost, and those that were willing to pay some price for a higher quality of life and the preservation of the earth's natural heritage; those which were concerned about the long-term future of mankind – a future which could not be clearly foreseen but must be provided for – and those that looked only at the immediate tasks facing their country and were willing to store up unknown problems for the future for the sake of resolving more quickly the known problems of the present. These were differences likely to feature increasingly prominently in the world's political system over the years to come.

TRANSNATIONAL POLITICS AND THE ENVIRONMENT

But political differences concerning the environment did not arise only among governments. There existed also a wide range of organizations, groups and individuals which had their own views and interests concerning that problem, quite independently of governments, and sought to exercise a direct influence on the action taken to confront it.

The groups involved are of a number of kinds. There are a huge number of national environmental organizations, some very specific in their concerns, some more general, some scientific, some political, of varying degrees of militancy and commitment, which are interested in lobbying their own national governments and mobilizing their own national public opinion on environmental questions. Usually they have mainly been concerned about the questions which directly affect their own state. With the rapid decline in distance, however, such groups have found, as have their governments, that many of the problems which concern them can be remedied only by international action. Even if their concern was primarily with the environment within their own country, they needed – since many threats came from elsewhere – to be able to influence action taken outside it too: by other governments or by international bodies with responsibilities in this field. As a result some of their campaigning and some of the representations they made (even when it was made to their own governments) concerned action which needed to be taken internationally.

They became almost as aware of threats to the ecologies of other countries as of those which existed in their own lands; they recognized that threats to species or resources were world-wide, not local problems, and thus came to care increasingly about threats to the planet as a whole (which is as much part of their environment as the soil, water and air within their own national frontiers). As a result national groups began to be linked to others in other lands sharing their own concerns, so that they came to act together on a global or at least a regional basis.

Such cooperation is of long standing. A number of national associations interested in the preservation of the bird population established, in London in 1922, the International Committee for Bird Preservation (later joined by an International Wildfowl Research Group). Naturalists and conservationists from many lands met regularly in international conferences for decades before they decided, in 1954, to set up an International Union for the Protection of Nature, which later became the International Union for the Conservation of Nature and Natural Resources (ICUN). This became the most important non-official body concerned with conservation. It was later largely responsible for formulating a World Conservation Strategy, published in 1980. There were a number of international scientific associations, of increasingly specialized kinds, which interested themselves in particular aspects of the question. The International Council of Scientific Unions (ICSU), for example, established a Scientific Committee on the Problems of the Environment. This has undertaken studies of particular environmental questions, including an important International Geosphere and Biosphere Programme. Other organizations have been rather less scientific and more political in their approach; for example, such bodies as the International Institute for the Environment and Development (IIED) which has issued reports on various aspects of the international environment, including that of the World Commission on Environment and Development (the Brundtland Report) proposing a wide-ranging programme designed to establish the concept of "sustainable", that is, environmentally responsible, development. More radical and militant are the campaigning organizations, which seek more far-reaching changes; in the policies of individual governments and international organizations alike. Some of these have been international from the beginning, such as Greenpeace; while the Friends of the Earth, which originated in the US, was within two years transformed into an international organization consisting of a federation of loosely linked international bodies.

Individuals wishing to influence the decisions which are important concerning international environment, therefore, find a considerable range of organizations which they can join or support. They can, if they wish, choose from among them the one that is most active on the issue of prime importance to them. If their main concern is the ending of whaling, they may choose to join or support Greenpeace;

if it is the conservation of the world's declining mineral resources, they may support ICUN, or one of its national constituents; if it is the preservation of animal species, the World Wildlife Fund; if it is the control or abolition of nuclear power production, or the prevention of acid rain, the Friends of the Earth. And so on. Just as, within national states, individuals join the political party, or single-issue organization, which most closely matches their own personal needs and beliefs, so in the wider international political system they can give their support to the non-governmental organizations which most closely match their views and concerns on global issues.

But can any of these bodies influence the decisions which matter: those reached within intergovernmental bodies? Mechanisms exist through which such unofficial organizations can seek to make their voices heard. Though the United Nations is primarily representative of governments, it was laid down at the time of its foundation that a place should be found, if only a modest one, for non-governmental organizations. It was laid down in Article 71 of the Charter that the Economic and Social Council, established as one of its principal bodies, might "make suitable arrangements for consultation with non-governmental organizations which are concerned with matters within its competence". The organizations concerned could be either international bodies or (so long as the member states concerned had been consulted) national organizations. An intergovernmental Committee on Non-governmental Organizations was set up within ECOSOC to determine which organizations were accepted and which rejected, and decide the status which they should be given.

The groups were divided into three separate categories, enjoying different degrees of access to the organization's affairs. The groups placed in Category A include trade unions and producer organizations, the Interparliamentary Union and the World Federation of United Nations Associations. Religious organizations, womens' groups and associations, development and welfare agencies were mainly placed in Category B. Groups concerned with particular occupations and recreations and campaigning groups were placed in Category C (now known as the roster). Some groups were recognized as being primarily interested in the work of one or more of the specialized agencies, and, if so recognized by the agency concerned, were automatically placed on the roster; while a few organizations were placed there by the UN Secretary-General using his personal authority. Only groups in Category A have the right to circulate documents to all delegates as official ECOSOC documents and to receive all circulated papers. They can even propose items for the agenda of the Council and have the right to speak on such questions as well as on some other items. Organizations placed in Category B can only have statements of less than 500 words distributed, and can speak only in certain committees, and then only with the permission of the NGO committee. There is thus something of a hierarchy of NGOs, and it can become a matter of considerable importance to an organization which category it is placed in. Such decisions are occasionally highly contentious: organizations undertaking activities which are unwelcome to some governments (such as Amnesty International) have sometimes had difficulty in retaining their status. To look after the interests of the NGOs and to resolve disputes among them, there exists an unofficial Conference of NGOs, based in New York and Geneva (CONGO), with a number of sub-committees concerned with particular subject areas.

These arrangements have not provided for NGOs the effective platform which they sought at the time of the UN's foundation. The activities of the NGOs have so far made little impact in the proceedings of the main UN bodies concerned with economic and social questions.[1] They have had rather more impact on subsidiary bodies: in the Human Rights Commission, for example, and especially in its Sub-commission and working groups, they are frequently given a respectful hearing; and sometimes have been a significant source of information and influence, which have affected the actions taken. A somewhat similar system for consulting NGOs exists within the EEC: NGOs, especially those representing trade unions, employers and consumers, are represented in the Economic and Social Committee, which discusses many issues in the areas of EEC competence. It is generally agreed, however, that it has almost no influence on the decisions reached.[2] In both the United Nations and the EEC informal contact with the secretariats of the organization probably provide a greater

1. According to one study "the consequences of the activities of many of the international NGOs are trivial. . . . They may serve in some degree to alter the domestic environment of decision-makers, but with some exceptions their effect either on capabilities or on objectives is likely to be minimal, and in no way can they be seen themselves as significant actors" (see B. A. Reynolds and R. D. McKinlay, 'The Concept of Interdependence: Its Uses and Misuses' in K. Goldman and G. Sjostedt (eds), *Power Capabilities and Inter-dependence Problems in Study of International Issues* (London, 1979) p. 154).
2. See J. Lodge and B. Herman, 'The Economic and Social Committee in EEC Decision-making', *International Organisation*, vol. 34, no. 2 (Spring 1980) p. 269. They conclude that the ESC plays a negligible role in EEC decision-making.

degree of influence than the formal machinery established. But even this is extremely limited.

NGOs concerned with the environment are naturally especially active in the organizations which operate in that area. The main focus of this activity is Nairobi, where UNEP is established. Unofficial organizations have established there an Environment Liaison Committee, which acts as a global network promoting exchange of information and joint action where appropriate.[3] It represents two or three hundred separate NGOs and maintains contact with about seven thousand others. It publishes a quarterly bulletin, reports regularly on the activities of UNEP and Habitat (the UN Centre for Human Settlements, also based in Nairobi), produces resource packs and other educational material, and seeks to coordinate joint activities. A similar body, the European Environment Bureau, has been established within the EEC. This represents nearly 70 NGOs within the EEC countries, has a small secretariat in Brussels and acts as a pressure group on environmental questions and a source of information about community affairs for its members. It has working parties dealing with the Common Agricultural Policy, energy, transport, toxic substances and other questions; organizes conferences and seminars on environmental questions; publishes a bi-monthly magazine and other publications; maintains contact with commission officials, and seeks to influence community policies which could have an impact on the environment. NGOs have also been active in lobbying the World Bank and other development agencies, trying to make them more aware of the environmental impact of their programmes. Partly as a result of these activities the principal development agencies now take part in the Committee of International Development Institutes on the Environment (CIDIE), within which these questions are discussed by the principal aid agencies.

A particular way in which NGOs have sought influence in recent times is by participating in parallel conferences, or Forums, organized to coincide with major international conferences among governments (p. 69 above). When the Stockholm Conference on the Environment

3. In 1973, in the aftermath of the Stockholm Conference, organizations concerned with environmental questions (including IIED, The Friends of the Earth and others) set up an International Assembly of Non-governmental Organizations Concerned with the Environment (INASEN). This in turn set up the Environment Liaison Board, which was given the responsibility for setting up a permanent centre for maintaining their activities. It was this which established the Environmental Liaison Committee, replacing the earlier organizations.

was being planned, international NGOs became active from an early stage, seeking to influence the agenda of the conference, and the type of outcome it should aim at. Members of the UN Secretariat and the Swedish government, which was hosting the conference, maintained continuing contacts with the organizations, kept them informed of the arrangements that were being made and listened to their views about the kind of outcome which should be aimed at. During the conferences, NGOs organized well-publicized meetings of their own, parallel to the official ones, and maintained continual contact with the official delegates. They published a daily newspaper, discussing the progress of the conference and the issues being discussed, which was delivered to the delegates, embassies, press centres and newspaper offices. As a result they secured almost as much coverage for the Forum as for the main conference. The precedent established on that occasion has been followed at subsequent international conferences: for example those on human habitations (in Canada in 1976); on population (in Romania in 1974); on womens' affairs (in Denmark in 1980); and at the special sessions on disarmament (in Geneva in 1978 and 1983).

It would be wrong to exaggerate the effect which any of these activities has had. But it would also be wrong to underestimate them. The decisions which are finally reached on such questions continue to be those of governments (even if of a number of governments acting together). Governments do not normally welcome, either at home or abroad, the activities of unofficial organizations. But the position taken up by governments may be affected, directly or indirectly (for example through influence on legislators or national officials), by the activities of the unofficial groups. Through their many contacts with international officials, they may sometimes influence the advice which these give. Through these various means they do probably finally have some impact on the actions which are taken when governments meet together. This is certainly as true on questions affecting the environment as on any other, if only because of the large number and loud voices of the organizations which are interested in that question.

The political process which is at work here is, however, not simply a confrontation between governments and environmental NGOs. For the environmental groups are in competition with other organizations which also seek to exercise an influence. Industrial associations, and even individual companies, are often at least as active; and they often seek decisions quite different from those demanded by the environmentalists. Their influence is usually hostile rather than favourable to further environmental regulation. Individual companies may lobby their own governments to resist the proposals put forward by the green campaigners. Thus, for example, ICI persuaded the British government to resist proposals for stricter controls on aerosols; just as the British electricity industry persuaded their government to resist demands for significiant modifications to power stations to prevent acid rain; and as the chemical industry in many countries resisted demands for more rigorous standards governing pesticides and the emission of chemical wastes. In reaching decisions on the policies they should adopt within the world body responsible, governments are obliged to take account of representations of both kinds. They are concerned about the effects of new controls on industrial competitiveness and on standards of living; as well as to respond to groups campaigning for higher environmental standards and quality of life. In choosing between them they will not always choose to heed the voice of the environmentalists.

Governments have to judge how far the groups which put particular points of view are representative of public opinion generally. They may defy the view put forward by the environmentalists on the ground that the latter represent the viewpoint of a relatively small minority of the deeply committed, rather than the viewpoint of public opinion generally. The same dilemma occurs at the global level. The representatives of poor countries, resisting a call for environmental standards which may slow industrialization, can argue that the NGOs which are most active in this field are based overwhelmingly in the richer countries of the world, and may represent the views that are current in those countries rather than in the world as a whole. It is the representatives of governments, contributing to decisions within each organization, that must finally decide how much account to take of the pressures that are exerted.

Unofficial organizations will nonetheless probably become an increasing influence on the decisions reached by international bodies in this area. They can at least be a source of information for those who reach the final decisions. They can mobilize public opinion for and against particular courses of action. And they will remain the principal channel through which those who do feel strongly about such questions can influence the decisions which are reached. Since the decisions that matter are increasingly those reached by international rather than by national bodies, lobbying and campaigning is likely to be increasingly on a world-wide basis. Increasingly, it will be recognized that on the emission of chemical wastes, the design of motor-car exhausts, the prevention of acid rain, the safety of nuclear reactors, the preservation of species and the protection of the biosphere, it will more and more be international decisions which count; international conventions, regulations and standards which will be demanded.

Though those concerned with these questions have had some success in raising international consciousness about the importance of the issues, internationally as well as nationally, many of their principal aims remain to be realized. Large numbers of natural species continue to become extinct; natural habitats are destroyed; forests continue to be cut down; disasters from chemical pollution or nuclear reactors continue to occur; monitoring of environmental degradation remains inadequate; and there is no adequate coordination of the many activities already undertaken within the UN family. If these challenges are to be adequately met, a central need, the campaigners recognize, is for more adequate funds to undertake the tasks required. More resources will need to be devoted to establishing an adequate system for monitoring changes in the world environment (on a scale far beyond that at present achieved by UNEP's Earthwatch programme). More help will be needed for global programmes, such as those against desertification, soil erosion and the destruction of forests. More assistance will have to be given to the many developing countries which are unable to undertake, from their own resources, many of the essential tasks required. More support will need to be given to the various programmes of specialized agencies in this field, and to regional initiatives, such as those devoted to cleaning up partially enclosed seas and encroaching deserts. To procure the resources required for these programmes, increasing attention will be demanded for the proposal, put forward in two major international reports of recent times – the Brandt and Brundtland reports – that a search should now be made for automatic sources of finance to replace the irregular and unpredictable contributions of governments: for example taxes on the principal users of threatened environments, such as the owners of oil tankers, ocean fishing and transportation companies, those who undertake seabed mining or seek to exploit Antarctic resources; charges on the use of space, for example, for communication satellites; taxes on air transport, international trade or trade of particular kinds; a special facility within the IMF, or specialized World Bank programmes, devoted to environmental purposes.

Ultimately the needs of the world environment may be held to demand a more explicit recognition of the duty of all states to safeguard their own share of the world's natural inheritance and to prevent damage being caused to other states (for example from acid rain, marine pollution or nuclear discharges). There will be pressure for renewed efforts to preserve endangered species, either by strengthening existing international legislation or ensuring that it is more widely ratified and respected. Adjustments in development policy to ensure that such programmes do not endanger the world's environment may be demanded. There may even be increasing recognition that simply to prevent the current deterioration in the world's environment from continuing may not be enough, and that often what is required is a reversal of damage already done: reforestation, restitution of damaged soil fertility, restocking of particular areas with species which have been driven out by previous policies. To achieve those purposes, it may be increasingly urged, UNEP may need to be made into a world-wide regulatory agency, comparable to similar bodies performing the same function within states.

Such steps can be taken only as a result of international rather than national action. For that reason effective political activity relating to the environment today can only take place at the global level. Because it is there, not in the relatively insignificant decisions of national states, that the important steps for safeguarding the world's threatened natural heritage must be taken, it is there too that in the future the significant political struggles will occur.

5 The Protection of Human Rights

There is another area of political concern that has increasingly required transnational rather than national action.[1]

A central part of all political activity has been the defence of the rights of the citizen. Writers on political theory have for hundreds of years discussed the limits to the power which should be wielded by governments over their populations. It has been widely argued that, even within their own frontiers, their claims on their people were not absolute but must be balanced against the rights of the individual citizens within these states. Increasingly it came to be maintained that there existed "fundamental" human rights which no government had the right to violate, and which should be respected and, if necessary, protected at all times. The defence of those rights became the aim of much political activity.

That action was for long taken within the context of national political systems alone. It was the right of individuals in the face of their *own* governments which was upheld. But over the last century or so such ideas have increasingly been applied internationally. It has come to be accepted that, where a government manifestly failed to respect the human rights of its own people, the governments and peoples of *other* states too had the right, and indeed the responsibility, to seek to secure their observance. Two centuries ago many joined the movement to bring about the abolition of slavery, in other states as well as their own, because that practice was seen to represent a denial of fundamental human freedoms which should be protected everywhere. With time this sense of an international responsibility has been extended. After the First World War similar world-wide movements sought to bring about the abolition of "white slavery" – the trade in prostitutes (p. 50 above) – and the observance of minimum labour rights throughout the international community.

But it was above all after 1945, after the atrocious violations of human rights which occurred in Nazi Germany, that it became widely accepted that international action was required to ensure that

1. The author is grateful to the editor of *International Affairs* for permission to use in this chapter material first published in an article in that journal.

individual rights were protected in every country in the world. Governments could no longer claim that the way they treated their own populations was a purely domestic concern, which was no business of those who lived elsewhere. National political systems were no longer trusted to safeguard individual rights adequately. The protection of human rights was increasingly seen as an international responsibility.

That responsibility has been undertaken partly by individual governments, seeking through bilateral action to influence the policies of other governments; partly by international organizations with responsibility in the area, seeking to influence the behaviour of their member-states; and partly by non-governmental organizations seeking to publicize and deter any violations that occurred anywhere in the world.

There are a number of difficulties which face any attempt by governments to play an active role in this field. Their concern to make an issue of human rights violations in another country may conflict with other important foreign policy aims. Every government needs to have dealings with most other governments of the world on many diverse questions. It must deal with them over the welfare of its own nationals, resident or trading abroad; over commercial and other practical problems which may arise; and over many wider issues affecting the international community as a whole. It will deal with them both bilaterally and in the United Nations and other international organizations. An active campaign designed to denounce the domestic policies of such a government to its own population will inevitably arouse deep resentment and will complicate dealings on any practical matter between the two states. It may endanger commercial or other prospects and the securing of government contracts. It will certainly damage political goodwill. And, since it will not necessarily bring any improvement in the human-rights situation in the country concerned in any case, it is understandable that many governments are reluctant to stick their necks out by intervening on such issues.

In some cases there may be more special reasons. The other state may be considered important for strategic reasons. It may even be an ally, so that to engage in criticism which might endanger the government's position may be held to be highly undesirable on defence grounds (it was these considerations which muted criticisms among other NATO governments of the Salazar regime in Portugal and that of the colonels in Greece, as well as some other governments in other parts of the world). Or the state concerned may be an important commercial partner. It may be an important supplier of raw materials, as South Africa is to all Western countries. It may be a financially powerful state which could make its displeasure felt in the foreign exchange markets; a consideration which, some believe, has virtually silenced criticism of Saudi Arabia and other oil-producing states in recent years. Finally, it may be a great power with which negotiations on many delicate subjects including vital strategic issues, are being undertaken.

Interference by a government on such matters was conventionally considered contrary to the rules of diplomatic intercourse. The tradition that each state exercises full sovereignty within its own territory precludes any criticism of the actions of other governments within their own countries. These rules, even if not always accepted by those nations wishing to make the criticisms, have been insisted on by those that are under criticism (so, for example, British governments of all political persuasions have consistently rejected the right of outside governments or organizations, and even of outside politicians, to make judgements on British policy in Northern Ireland). How much more, it is argued, will authoritarian governments – often guilty of gross brutality towards their own subjects – reject any attempt by outsiders to influence their conduct? If every government began criticizing and commenting on all actions of every other government in every part of the world, even those it undertakes within its own territory – offering perhaps conflicting advice – the conduct of international affairs would, under this view, become impossible.

Finally, it is said that such efforts are in any case ineffectual: they will have no influence. They are thus a waste of energy, resources and political capital. The type of government that engages in oppression of basic human freedoms is often already intensely insecure and is unlikely to be deterred from its policies by criticism from other governments. Indeed, for such a government it may be a point of honour to ignore all criticism: to demonstrate its own independence and its unwillingness to be deterred. Harsh penalties may be imposed as a demonstration that that government cannot be deflected from its chosen course by outside criticism. Finally, it is argued that overt criticisms on such questions, by alienating the government concerned, may in fact serve to *reduce* the influence of the outside governments which advance them, and make it less likely that they can have any useful impact in similar situations in the future.

Over recent years all these arguments have come to carry less and less weight. It is of course the case that any government is obliged to deal on a day-to-day basis with many other governments, whether or not it approves of them, on a large number of different and mainly uncontroversial issues. Most of these relations will continue, whatever posture that government may adopt on human-rights issues. It is unreasonable to expect that relations will be totally unaffected. If the complaints made are aired in a polemical and highly political style, or are pursued obsessively and to the exclusion of all other questions, the relationship may be damaged. If, on the other hand, the complaint made is raised in the proper forum, in reasonable terms, and is consistent with the policy pursued on similar matters towards other states, this need not be the case.

The fact that human-rights issues have already in the last few years become so much the normal stuff of international politics has reduced the danger that any expression of concern on such matters can be used by other governments as a justification for breaking off or damaging relations. No individual government can any longer insulate itself altogether from this change in the international climate. Even the Soviet Union today submits to questioning on its domestic policies in the Human-Rights Committee (which supervises the implementation of the Covenant on Civil and Political Rights). It and nearly all other states gladly participate elsewhere in the discussion of the human-rights policies of South African, Chilean and Israeli governments, and rightly reject any attempt by the governments of those countries to claim immunity on the grounds of domestic sovereignty. It is thus now almost universally recognized that serious violations of human rights are a matter of concern to the international community as a whole. And while the states accused will doubtless continue to protest when other governments criticize their record in this field, it is less and less likely that interstate relations will be fatally damaged.

Even the governments that are most fiercely criticized do not in practice fatally disrupt relationships in retaliation. Even at the time when American criticism of Soviet human-rights policies was at its height, the Soviet Union continued to discuss SALT and many other matters as before. Criticisms of South Africa's policies of apartheid or Israel's policies in the occupied territories has not prevented governments which have made them from maintaining relatively normal relations with those governments on other questions. There is, in other words, a considerable willingness to divorce disagreements on such matters from the conduct of affairs in other areas. It cannot, of course, be said that no price will be paid for being outspoken: this is the price of having a human-rights policy. But it is not usually an unduly heavy one.

There is therefore no reason why governments that feel strongly on such questions should not make their views known. The reason why governments generally refrain from speaking out on such questions is that it is inconvenient to do so, not because it is fatally damaging. It is not believed to be worthwhile to create difficulties in relations with important states for ends that are regarded, by most officials and by many ministers, as only marginal in importance. How far a government will in practice go in criticizing a friendly or politically important state about human-rights usually depends on the degree to which public opinion at home demands it, rather than on the absolute scale of its atrocities. British governments did not hesitate to express their condemnation of policies of, for example, the Soviet Union, Uganda, Chile and South Africa, because public opinion at home demanded it. They spoke out less strongly about the policies of Equatorial Guinea, the Central African Republic, Uruguay, Cuba, China and Ethiopia, because public opinion and even human-rights organizations did not express themselves as strongly on that subject, not because it was thought important not to prejudice relations with those states.

The international climate has therefore changed radically. It is no longer accepted that the expression of concern by governments on human rights questions is contrary to the traditional rules of diplomatic intercourse. These rules have changed quite dramatically in the last 30 or 40 years. In the UN Charter provision was explicitly made for the discussion of human-rights matters in the organization, and in its Commission on Human Rights in particular. This has been reinforced by the subsequent establishment of regional organizations devoted to the same subject, such as the European Commission and Court of Human Rights and the InterAmerican Commission on Human Rights, and subsequently in such documents as the Helsinki Final Act – which has clear references to human-rights issues. And it is shown above all in the current practice of states many of which (not all developed countries) continually make clear the importance they attach to the conduct of other governments in this respect.

It would be wrong to expect bilateral representations to have dramatic effects. Few realistic observers expect that, because one or two governments begin to state their concern about the human-rights situation in a particular state the government of that country is suddenly going to reverse all its policies and become at once a model of virtue. In the short term, little may happen. But there may be indirect effects. First, the government under attack may be gradually brought to realize that there are significant external costs to the type of policy it is pursuing. At least its foreign office, which is usually most aware of foreign criticisms, may become an influence within the government machine for a reform of policy. Secondly, human-rights campaigners within the country concerned may be given new hope and encouragement, and redouble their own efforts to secure reforms. Changes may be induced within the government itself, with those favouring a more liberal policy (partly because of its foreign policy effects) prevailing over those furthering repressive policies (as has occurred in South Africa). But above all, the international climate as a whole will be altered. The expectations that are placed on all members of the international community are slowly changed. New norms of the behaviour to be expected from civilized governments are established. Regional organizations that may previously have been ineffective in this field may become more active. It is this wider effect, the slowest and most indirect of all, which may none the less ultimately be the most important in reducing the scale of human-rights violations, for ultimately it will affect the expectations and attitudes of all: even those of *future* governments which might otherwise be tempted towards tyrannical policies.

The change in assumptions has freed governments from their former apathy. The inhabitants of different states are no longer seen as living in totally separate, watertight compartments, beyond the reach of those elsewhere. It is now widely recognized that governments have both the right and the responsibility to seek to ensure respect for human rights in other countries.

But however deeply committed they may be to securing those goals (and many are not), individual governments acting in isolation have limited influence. Each is constrained in what it can do by its own foreign policy goals, commercial considerations, political sympathies or traditional friendships. The influence any single government can have on the state which is violating human rights will anyway be weak. The role of individual governments in this area, therefore, though not insignificant, is limited.

Alternative sources of influence, more broadly based and more impartial, and so more likely to be effective in restraining oppressive action by other governments have, therefore, increasingly been sought.

THE ROLE OF INTERNATIONAL ORGANIZATIONS

Since 1945 it has been accepted that, to secure effective protection of human rights, multi-lateral measures too are necessary. The appalling violations of human rights which occurred under totalitarian governments in the previous decade brought a determination that the new organization established to maintain the peace of the world in the post-war period should also be given responsibility for trying to secure respect for human rights in all member-states.

The principal body established for that purpose was the UN Commission on Human Rights, which, together with its two sub-committees, was to operate under the general supervision of the Economic and Social Council (ECOSOC) and the General Assembly. The Commission spent most of its early years in devising grandiloquent Declarations, Conventions and Covenants, designed to set out in abstract terms the rights which governments were expected to respect. It took no steps to secure observance of the commitments made. Most governments had no hesitation in putting their signatures to many high-minded undertakings, while continuing to violate, with persistent brutality, the very rights they undertook to protect.

Though the Commission has on these grounds been criticized with some reason in the past, there has been a significant improvement in its operation in recent years. It has come to be widely recognized within the Commission that what really counts is deeds and not words, and that therefore what is now required is better machinery to ensure that governments abide by their undertakings. This has been shown in two ways. When new instruments have been negotiated it has been laid down from the start in one or two cases that there should be some machinery for supervising implementation. This was done for the Convention for the Elimination of Racial Discrimination (1965); and, more importantly, for the Covenant on Civil and Political Rights, which came into effect in 1976. In both cases intergovernmental committees were set up which cross-examine representatives of each government on its performance in putting the instrument into effect, and subsequently issues a report. The necessity to justify themselves before these committees, and the danger of being exposed if it has been shown they are flagrantly failing to live up to their obligations, probably represent some influence on governments (as do the similar procedures employed by the ILO over many years for covenants concerning labour standards). Minorities within the state concerned are also able to quote the terms of the undertaking which their government has made. And the procedures serve to establish more unmistakably than written documents alone the standards of national conduct which are expected by the international community.

The other, and perhaps more important, development is the use of the so-called 1503 procedure (named after the UN Economic and Social Council resolution which first established it). This is a procedure under which the human-rights situation in particular countries may be examined by the Commission. The procedure is long and cumbrous, beginning in a working group of the sub-commission (which meets in August/September); the case is then passed on to the sub-commission, which may and often does recommend action by the Commission; it then goes to another working group (of the Commission itself), which finally makes a further recommendation to the Commission. The number of hurdles to be crossed has meant that very few issues have got all the way through to substantive discussion and decision by the Commission. Moreover, all the discussion is, at least in theory, confidential – though in practice there are often judicious leaks at least about which countries have been discussed (so that the procedure may have some effect even if it never reaches its final conclusion). However, public discussion is also possible by other procedures. The situation in Chile, South Africa and the territories occupied by Israel have all been discussed in open debates. The former Labour government in Britain raised the situations in Uganda and Cambodia in public debate in the Commission; and in both cases eventually some form of international action ensued, though it is symptomatic of the very slow-moving machinery that in each case the offending government was overthrown before any substantive action was taken.

Thus the procedure is still inadequate, but it is a beginning. Today resolutions are passed in the General Assembly about the human-rights situation in particular countries. This represents a significant advance on the situation when UN bodies discussed human-rights only in abstract terms and never concerned themselves with the situations that actually existed in particular countries. At that time communications and petitions were all pigeonholed and never discussed: now the many communications received are examined to see if they give evidence of a "systematic pattern of gross violations of human rights". The task now is to build on what has been developed. It is necessary, for example, to try to speed up the whole procedure so that it can reach final conclusions much earlier: otherwise, as in the case of Uganda, Equatorial Guinea and others, discussion will proceed interminably while thousands of lives are being lost, so that nothing is actually done until the regime has finally fallen. There is also a case for allowing public *reports* to be made by the sub-commission, and perhaps by its working group, even if the *debates* remain confidential. It would be valuable to call more senior representatives of governments to appear at the Commission more often. Above all it is necessary to establish better fact-finding machinery so that reports concerning the position on the spot may be made by impartial observers (like the studies made by the InterAmerican Commission on Human Rights). Sub-commissions could perhaps be appointed to look at individual situations; and there could be a role for regional field officers.

There should also be more frequent meetings of the Commission (at least twice a year) so that urgent questions could more easily be raised; or at least the establishment of a small sub-commission that could meet at more frequent intervals and in emergencies. Above all, there should be much more publicity for the Commission's activities, so that the healthy fear that governments are already beginning to have of its reports, manifested in the intensive lobbying they undertake to prevent adverse reports (as by the Argentine government in the late seventies), is intensified. This is a matter primarily for the media, but the United Nations itself can do something through its Office of Public Information. Non-governmental organizations can also play a vitally important part in focusing more attention on the Commission's work.

There is another development of the existing machinery which could be of value. There is no doubt that governments are sometimes more influenced by the judgements of bodies which represent governments in their own immediate neighbourhood, of similar political and cultural background. Already in Latin America the InterAmerican Commission on Human Rights probably plays a more effective part in judging and deterring human-rights violations there than any UN body. Similarly, the European Commission and Court have been entrusted with much greater power by its member governments than has the UN Commission because they trust its judgement. The step that would perhaps do more than anything else to improve the protection of human rights in the world today would thus be the creation of effective bodies to perform the same role in Africa and Asia.

The Organization of African Unity approved a Charter on Human and Peoples' Rights in 1982. As this title made clear, the document demonstrated a greater concern for the rights of entire peoples (such as those in South Africa) than of individuals. It nonetheless represented a substantial advance on anything which previously existed: The Charter came into effect in 1987 when the Commission on Human Rights which it established began operating. In Asia, though there has been some discussion about the setting up of such a Commission, no significant steps have been taken, and the human rights situation remains poor even in some states purporting to be democratic.

There has been a great deal of discussion in the United Nations over many years about the establishment of a High Commissioner for Human Rights. The establishment of an authoritative figure, who could, whenever he received strong *prima facie* evidence of violations of human rights, ask to examine the situation on the spot and subsequently report, would clearly be a valuable innovation. The difficulty is that, in this form at least, the proposal has become something of a political football. It has been supported mainly by Western countries and is seen by some developing countries and even more by the Communist states as evidence of a desire by the West to interfere in their internal affairs. Many countries do not welcome the prospect of a close examination of their arrangements by such a figure. Any proposal that is to have a chance of success must take account of these apprehensions. Though it would be possible for those governments willing to accept the proposal to go ahead by themselves, and hope to draw in others as the system developed, this could probably not be done under the auspices of the United Nations and there is some danger in creating a divided system. For the moment it might be better to settle for a figure with more modest powers, such as the "Co-ordinator of Human Rights Affairs" that has been suggested by Nigeria. Even an upgrading of the post of Head of the Human Rights Division in Geneva to enable him to use his authority more assertively from time to time would do something. But it would help even more if the Secretary-General would lend his own considerable authority to seeking solutions of particularly glaring human-rights violations on occasions.

What should be the general objectives of the international bodies working in this field?

The first aim of any organization concerned with human-rights is to ensure that it remains at the top, or near the top, of the international agenda. The easiest policy to pursue in this field is to remain silent. Because the whole question is so controversial, governments are inevitably tempted to conclude that discretion is the better part of valour and simply keep quiet on the subject. Because governments deal with other governments, the temptation is not to offend them too much, whatever the shortcomings in their conduct. But, if the question is as important as many people believe, and if governments are willing to prejudice their bilateral relationships with the government concerned then it is all the more important that international bodies continue to make human rights an important international issue and ensure that they are kept at the forefront of international attention.

A second important aim must be to ensure that the minimum standards of human rights which civilized states expect to see observed are satisfactorily defined. The essential standards by which governments must be judged were first laid down, in somewhat general terms, in the Universal Declaration of Human Rights, formulated in 1946 and endorsed by almost the entire international community. Since then these have been amplified in more detailed and specific instruments, mainly formulated in the UN Commission on Human Rights. The most important of these are perhaps, respectively, the two Covenants on civil and political rights and on economic, social and cultural rights – the former of which has now come into effect. There are also more specialized instruments covering particular fields, such as the convention on all forms of racial discrimination, and that still being discussed on religious tolerance. There are also special regional codes such as those established in the European Convention and applied by the European Commission and Court of Human Rights, and that operated by the InterAmerican Commission on Human Rights. One of the continuing aims of governments working in this field is to clarify and amplify this code, particularly by extending it in certain specialized areas.

Since any instrument in this field must, if it is to have any influence, reflect the views of the international community generally, it can only emerge from a process of international negotiation. At present this work is done sometimes by working groups of the Commission on Human Rights or (as in the case of the Covenants) by the Commission itself, followed by detailed examination in the Third Committee of the General Assembly. It cannot really be said that such bodies, with fairly low-level representatives often with little or no legal background, are well equipped for this difficult but very important task. It really requires a forum that is legal rather than political in its approach. There is a case for asking the International Law Commission (which is anyway less directly representative of governments) to be more closely involved in the process in the future. Though it has undertaken the drafting of a number of extremely important conventions, the Commission – composed of distinguished international lawyers from a balanced group of countries – has not taken any part in drafting conventions in the field of human rights. Since it is balanced by nationality, like all UN bodies, it would reflect as well as they do the varying national approaches to such questions. But it will not be so influenced by narrowly political factors as purely intergovernmental bodies sometimes are.

There are a number of specific areas where new instruments of this kind are required. Over recent years there have been important debates concerning new rules governing the rights of mental patients (it is well known that it is a common practice in certain countries to incarcerate troublesome dissidents by declaring them mentally disordered), as well as rules governing the treatment of all those under detention, the rights of the child, the right to privacy and other previously neglected areas. All of these are important questions – central issues for the protection of human rights – and it is vital that satisfactory texts should be achieved which can significantly influence the behaviour of governments in these areas. It is particularly important that the new international convention covering torture, one of the most hideous yet most widely used violations of human rights in recent years, should be widely ratified. But efforts to improve penal practice generally are also required. Although, for example, imprisonment without trial is often regarded as one of the most serious violations of human rights that can occur, it is widespread; and there are many countries all over the world, including some with otherwise good human-rights records (such as India and Italy), where people, subsequently found to be perfectly innocent, may languish in jail for many years before being brought to trial at all.

A third aim of international bodies must be to try to ensure that adequate machinery exists to see the new codes are complied with. It is generally accepted that the UN bodies responsible should now move on from legislation to the process often described as "implementation": ensuring that governments adequately conform with the good intentions which they have professed. Improvement of the machinery to achieve this is by no means easy because of the resistance of many members to granting the United Nations effective powers in this field. This results partly from a general sensitivity about sovereignty – a reluctance to see any interference by international bodies in domestic matters – and partly from the fact that many governments have skeletons in their own cupboard and recognize that if more effective machinery were created it could well be applied against themselves. But there should as a minimum be further attempts to secure the appointment of a UN High Commissioner for Human Rights.

The fourth aim of human-rights bodies must be to bring direct influence to bear on governments all over the world so that the grave violations of human rights, which unhappily remain only too common, become less likely to occur. As we have seen, this is both the most important and the most difficult task. Governments are often indifferent to the recommendations of international bodies. Often they may believe that their own survival depends on the continuation of policies of repression: that they face a "security" problem which requires that "subversive" forces should be suppressed. In these circumstances, even if they recognize that serious violations of human rights are occurring, they may feel that these are the inevitable cost of maintaining power, or bringing a disturbed situation under control (this has for instance been the main justification used for human-rights violations in Argentina, Uruguay and some other Latin American countries in recent times). Or, even worse, they may, like an Amin or a Pol Pot, care absolutely nothing for the opinions of other countries, any more than they do for that of their own people, and thus appear almost totally impervious to any representations or appeals that other states may make. But, whatever the motives or attitudes of such governments, it is an essential aim of human-rights bodies to bring effective influence to bear to secure a reversal of policy.

Should equal standards be demanded on this question from all other governments?

It is sometimes suggested that Western countries, in the insistent emphasis they place on human-rights matters are, at least in their dealings with third-world states, seeking to impose on countries of totally different cultures and conditions attitudes and standards developed in the West for Western societies, which are in no way appropriate for universal application. It is held that there are no absolute standards in this field, and that it is only comparatively recently that Western countries themselves have begun to conform with the principles which they now preach so ardently. They thus have no right to seek to apply them to others of widely differing backgrounds. For poor countries, it is said, human rights begin with breakfast. What matters to them is that people should have enough to eat and to house and clothe their families. The civil and political liberties to which Western countries attach such importance, therefore, are an irrelevance which have little meaning for such countries.

The argument is a gross and unwarranted insult to the poor countries that it purports to defend. When we speak of human rights we are speaking of the elementary right of people not to be killed, not to be tortured, not to be arbitrarily imprisoned, not to be raped or assaulted. Those rights are not a recent discovery but have been recognized the world over almost from the beginning of time. The belief in such rights is not the invention of the Western world but is cherished equally in the third world. There are a considerable number of poor countries (particularly in the Pacific, in the Caribbean and parts of Africa and Asia) which have consistently maintained the very highest standards of human rights despite a very low standard of living (just as there are some wealthy countries that none the less have extremely poor records in this respect). But, if it is an insult to the governments and people of those countries which have good records to suggest that human rights standards should not be applied to poor countries, it is even more of an insult to the hundreds of thousands, and possible millions, who have suffered violations of their rights, who have lost their lives in Cambodia and Uganda, or been tortured in Latin America, to imply, however indirectly, that the governments of such countries cannot be expected to refrain from killing or torturing them because of the low standard of living there. Arguments on these lines indeed – apart from being factually false – could be used to provide a heaven-sent justification to tyrants and petty officials or military officers in poor countries who wish to find excuses for their repressive policies. It is not the case – and fortunately is not accepted as the case in most developing countries – that poverty excuses or condones barbarous conduct by governments there.

Nor is there, as such arguments imply, in some way a choice to be made between economic rights and civil rights. Both sets of rights are of the highest importance. They are in no way in conflict with each other. Development is not impeded in a society which respects human rights. Indeed, the evidence would seem to prove the contrary. In general the developing countries which have shown the highest respect for human rights have the best record of economic growth. And, conversely, it is in states where human rights have been most widely and systematically abused – in such countries as Cambodia. Equatorial Guinea, the Central African Republic, Haiti, Ethiopia and Burma – that economic growth has been slowest, if it has not indeed been backward.

The two types of rights, therefore, far from being in conflict, are complementary. It is the governments that are genuinely concerned about the economic standard of living of their people that usually have most concern about their rights in other fields as well: while, conversely, it is those that are least concerned about their civil rights that will neglect their economic rights. It is a legitimate argument for third-world countries to use against the West that, if they are concerned about human rights at all, they should be concerned about economic rights as well (and therefore be willing to provide more aid and better access to their markets). It is not a legitimate argument that, because economic rights are important, civil rights can be ignored.

Fortunately this is a truth generally recognized by most third world countries. Nothing has been more heartening during recent years than to note the importance attached to this subject by many third-world states – as evidenced, for example, in the leading role played by a number of them (including Senegal, Nigeria, Sierra Leone, Lesotho and India) in the Human Rights Commission. Indeed there is a case for saying that Western countries should, as far as possible, leave the task of highlighting the violations that occur in parts of the third world to other developing countries – thereby avoiding the charge of neo-colonial imperialism. The standards they apply, however, will be those that are generally applied to the international community as a whole. It is not by chance that the most important international instrument in this field is entitled the *Universal* Declaration of Human Rights, and was adopted without a single dissentient vote. The assertion was that the standards laid down could and should be attained in any country. It was never accepted that any state is too small, too remote or too poor to be expected to attain them.

THE ROLE OF NON-GOVERNMENTAL ORGANIZATIONS

But there is a limit to what international bodies can achieve in this field. Their actions will always reflect the attitudes and opinions of the governments represented within them. Those governments are themselves not necessarily representative of the views of individuals, within their own states or elsewhere. The same timidity, the same concern to avoid antagonizing other governments, which inhibits their own actions towards other states will equally inhibit the actions they take as members of international organizations. If human rights in other countries are to be more adequately protected, therefore, a vital role must be played by non-governmental organizations and private individuals concerned about such questions.

The importance of the role which these play does not derive only from their independence. It derives also from the fact that they may have more opportunity for direct contact and direct influence than either governments or international organizations can have. They may, for example, be directly in contact with those in other countries whose rights are being abused, in a way that the representatives of governments seldom are. Diplomats abroad, perhaps because they are dealing on a day-to-day basis with a particular set of rulers, tend to become gradually committed to existing regimes and acquire a marked reluctance to take any steps which may be unwelcome to them. For the same reason they are most unwilling to have contact with groups or organizations that are regarded by those authorities as "subversive". These are constraints which do not affect non-governmental organizations.

Such organizations are able to speak, and certainly to publish, their concern more freely than governments can do. They are less likely to be accused of political bias, or a desire to score points off a political opponent. And they are more likely to be accepted as reflecting and representing the opinions of ordinary people everywhere. Governments can provide assistance for such groups. Financial assistance would not usually be welcomed by them, since they would feel that their independence could be prejudiced, or at least that this might be believed. But there can be regular exchanges of information and ideas, a pooling of knowledge about the situation in particular states; joint seminars or other activities to educate the public; and cooperation in international human-rights bodies. Human-rights organizations can also establish regular contacts with parliamentary committees on foreign affairs, to ensure that their members, in considering policy towards particular countries and areas, are at all times conscious of the human-rights consideration involved. Parliamentarians, and indeed governments, are usually concerned to reflect the views of influential and active groups within the nation; and, the more frequent and regular their contacts with human-rights bodies, the more such concerns are likely to be reflected in policy.

A vital need these organizations can fulfil is to provide reliable information about the human rights violations occurring all over the world. World-wide there has probably been some small improvement in respect for human rights since the dark days of Pol Pot, Amin, Nguema, Somoza and other tyrants. But these welcome improvements should not obscure the fact that in those places brutal violations of human rights, including the indiscriminate slaughter of innocent people, could occur over years without any effective action by the international community – indeed, to some extent almost unregarded by the outside world. After the defeat of Nazi Germany and the revelation of the unspeakable crimes commited there, many people said that never again would the world sit idly by while millions of innocent people were brutally slaughtered by an insane government. Yet in Cambodia this is precisely what occurred again between 1975 and the end of 1978, while the rest of the world did precisely nothing and few governments uttered a single word of protest. If equally monstrous happenings were to begin elsewhere next year, would the world again stand by, equally dumb and equally inactive?

One thing that is necessary therefore if human-rights organizations are to be more successful in the future is that more information should be made available to the public about the situation that exists in different countries all over the world. At present, though most educated people have a vague idea of what is happening in individual countries, impressions are generally unclear: based on stray newspaper reports rather than reliable and systematically compiled evidence. In practice the degree of concern that is felt about each situation depends almost entirely on how far it happens to have been highlighted by the press and television. Because there was widespread reporting in Britain about the situation in Uganda between 1975 and 1979, there was general concern in Britain about that country; because there was none about Equatorial Guinea, there was little concern and almost no knowledge, about the situation there, though the situation measured in the number of totally innocent people slaughtered was almost certainly worse. Similarly, because there were only a few and scattered reports about the situation in Cambodia, there was only slight and sporadic public concern about it at the time when large-scale killings were taking place; and opinion became generally aroused only when the government responsible had already fallen and television programmes began showing the starvation of the population left behind. Even the best-known human-rights organizations in Britain during that time devoted far more of their resources to publicizing the situation in Chile and Argentina and the Soviet Union: situations which, bad though they were, cannot be compared with the situation of prolonged and systematic slaughter that was occurring in Cambodia and Equatorial Guinea.

If outside opinion, including that represented by non-governmental organizations is to be able to play a more effective role in preventing such outrages from occurring again, it is essential that the public should be equipped with more objective information about the situations that exist all over the world, and the relative scale of the violations that are occurring. Governments usually only take action when public opinion is aroused in their own countries; and a better-informed public opinion could do much to stimulate more effective action by governments. The most useful action that could be taken – perhaps by Amnesty or the human-rights network working together – would be the publication of an annual survey of the human-rights situation in every country in the world (or at the very least all those where human rights are being seriously violated), with some indication of the gravity of the situation in each place. This would not necessarily involve a system of marking though it would require fairly bold judgements about the scale of the threats to human life and liberty that were occurring in each state. But it would involve a systematic collation of press reports, and of first-hand accounts from those on the spot in each country. It would need to be done on a systematic and highly objective basis. But it should not be beyond the capability or resources of the organizations working in this field. It would magnify many times the value of the periodic reports at present issued about individual countries, because it would present a comprehensive picture of the world situation so far as human-rights violations are concerned; it would give people an idea of the relative seriousness of the problems in different countries of the world; and it would serve to remind people of the continuing problems existing in countries that had not perhaps been reported on individually for some years. It would not only be of assistance to all unofficial organizations and individual workers in this field. It would assist governments in showing them where they should best direct their own efforts without being accused of political partiality.

One of the main roles of unofficial groups is in strengthening the backbone of their own governments. It is governments which will have the greatest influence on those responsible for human rights violations but, as we have seen, they face real problems in giving expression to their concern. When all that is involved is the passage of resolutions and the drafting of conventions, the problems are not great. When it is necessary to move on from that process to seeking to influence the conduct of rulers elsewhere towards their own populations in their own territories many governments feel constrained to pull their punches: because of the danger, in their own eyes, of prejudicing their relations. These attitudes derive partly from the narrow way in which national interests are conceived. The wider and more long-term national interests – in bringing about a world in which fewer people are killed, tortured or imprisoned without reason and more enjoy basic freedoms, including freedom to have a say in the way they are governed; even the less noble one of securing the gratitude of future governments once the oppressive regime has been overthrown, while winning world respect for the demonstration of concern on these questions – count for little against the immediate aim of not offending existing governments. A little human-rights training for diplomats, or at least intensive briefing on the question before each foreign posting, would be a help; there is little in the current training of diplomats to lead them to take much interest in this subject. Only if these wider aims come to play a much larger role than they have in the past will governments begin to become more active in the protection of human rights elsewhere.

One of the major tasks for NGOs concerned with these matters is to ensure that these wider considerations play the role that they should in government thinking. It is important that such organizations maintain and deepen their links with governments, so that the latter can be made fully aware of the importance that the public, outside official circles, attach to the issue. They should seek to foster contacts with officials as well as with ministers (since the former are at least as important in formulating policy); and should insist that they see sometimes the most senior officials, rather than the comparatively junior bureaucrats with whom they often have to be content to deal at present. They should continue to maintain close links with MPs and seek to mobilize these as an effective pressure on governments: parliamentary opinion in Britain, for instance, has so far been a much more muted forces in such matters than the human-rights lobby in the UN Congress.

Finally, the NGOs have a vital role to play in educating opinion at large; including opinion in other countries, and especially in the third world, where there is a less strong tradition of interest in such matters. The organization of conferences, seminars and other activities, the publication of suitable literature and the maintenance of links with corresponding organizations in other countries all have a role to play here. In the final resort, better respect for human rights everywhere can only be brought about through changing the attitudes of world public opinion, and so changing the climate of expectations which ultimately influence governments.

The willingness of governments to play an active role in influencing the human-rights situation in other countries will ultimately depend on the demands placed upon them by their own public opinion. The extent to which, therefore, human-rights considerations play a significant part in the foreign policy of those governments will depend crucially on the success of the NGOs and individuals in building up a wider recognition, at home and abroad, of the importance of these issues; a recognition that, in today's narrow world torture and sudden death is the concern of all of us, in whatever territory we may happen to dwell.

In the human-rights field, as in others, therefore, international society has become a single, closely interrelated organism. The actions each government takes towards its own population cannot be kept in isolated compartments, unknown to those elsewhere and unregarded by them. All today care about the way their fellow-creatures are treated by those in authority, whether they live within their own national frontiers or beyond them.

Gross violations of rights are therefore no longer domestic but global issues. And only global political action is an adequate response to them.

6 The Distribution of Economic Power

ECONOMIC INEQUALITIES IN THE MODERN WORLD

Another type of political aim which can only, in the modern world, be achieved globally rather than nationally is action to bring about a more just distribution of economic power.

Political action has always been deeply concerned with that aim. Many have thought economic inequalities to be as important as political inequalities. They have often been seen as their cause. Many early reformers, in denouncing the selfishness and greed of the rich and powerful, demanded that, if political justice was to be secured, there must be a more equal sharing of wealth and income in society. Socialist thinkers in more recent times have stressed the need for a more just distribution of property as a precondition for establishing a more just society generally. Karl Marx, seeing the distribution of property as the most fundamental factor determining the economic and social situation of individuals, believed that only a fundamental transformation of property rights would be successful in transforming the political situation of disadvantaged sections of society. Socialist politicians have therefore demanded a transfer of property to the state, so that it might be able to ensure that it was used productively for the benefit of all, and would enable the people to enjoy the fruits of their labour. And socialists and non-socialists alike regarded the development of welfare services and the creation of the welfare state as the means of securing a fairer distribution of wealth and welfare throughout society. Whether it was believed that economic changes would bring political power for the majority or, on the contrary, that an increase in their political power, for example through the extension of the franchise, would be the means of securing a fairer distribution of resources, a reduction in economic inequality was seen by many as the essential condition for creating a more just society.

That concern, however, was always with a single society. It was justice and equality within the state which was at issue. It was only this, it was believed, which political action could influence. A wider equality was not seen as within the realm of political power or political discussion.

The demand for equality was not accepted by all. Others believed that economic inequality was the condition of progress. An equal society, such people argued, would be a stagnant society. Inequality was necessary to provide the incentive that would alone secure the effort needed to bring about the efficient running of a complex, modern economic system. Inequalities were not only needed as the dynamic force promoting desirable change. They also reflected the judgement of society concerning the relative contribution made by different groups and individuals to its successful performance. Since some positions in society demanded greater skill, experience, responsibility or authority, it was right that they should command a higher rate of remuneration. Even the acquisition of property, it was sometimes held, was the result of enterprise or "abstinence"; and it too should therefore secure a reasonable return. It was right that rewards should be distributed according to effort and ability. A society in which inequality existed would therefore not only be more efficient but more just.

These traditional justifications of inequality were not always found convincing. Was it true that inequality was a necessary incentive? Were not positions of responsibility and the exercise of skill anyway always preferred to positions of lower status, responsibility and authority? Would they not therefore readily be taken up without any special incentive in the form of higher remuneration? Under this view they neither required nor deserved the vastly higher salaries which they normally enjoy today. On the contrary, it was the most arduous and undesirable positions such as those of dustmen, building labourers, agricultural workers and domestics – at present very poorly paid – which were most arduous and unattractive and therefore most deserved higher remuneration. The alleged incentive effect of higher incomes was anyway totally irrelevant for most people, since it was not open to the vast majority of the population – teachers, office workers, bus conductors and many others – to increase their productivity according to the amount they were paid. Nor was promotion to a position of higher responsibility (and pay) an available option for them: the great majority of people were likely to spend the rest of their working lives in the same level of employment as that which they occupied in their twenties. Finally, a large proportion of the most important advantages of wealth were enjoyed not by those who acquired them but by second and third generations who had done nothing whatever to deserve special privileges, but enjoyed preferential education, cultural and other career opportunities as a result of inheriting advantages earned by their forebears.

Within states these questions have been the stuff of political argument for many years. The relative weight to be attached to the two points of view cannot be determined on purely rational grounds: they depend ultimately (like all arguments concerning "justice") on subjective choices. Differences about the relative importance to be attached to efficiency or equity, the reward for success or compensation for need, are not susceptible of proof. They cannot therefore be definitively resolved. The best that can be done is to provide relevant evidence and argument, on the basis of which personal judgements can be made.

What is certain, however, is that whatever the arguments adduced for and against inequalities within states, they are irrelevant to the most significant inequalities of the modern world: those which exist between individuals in different states. Whatever arguments may be found to show that a judge in Britain deserves ten times the salary and way of life of a schoolteacher, it is difficult to argue that a judge in Britain deserves ten times the salary and way of life of a judge in Bangladesh; that a schoolteacher in Britain deserves ten times the salary of a schoolteacher in Bangladesh. Whether or not the responsibility (or skill) which a judge exercises is ten times greater than that of a schoolteacher, the responsibility (or skill) of a judge in Britain can scarcely be ten times that of a judge performing an exactly similar role for a similar area in Bangladesh. Whether or not the work of a schoolteacher is more arduous and highly trained than that of an agricultural worker, that of a schoolteacher (or agricultural worker) in Britain can scarcely be ten times more arduous and highly trained than that of those undertaking the same tasks in Bangladesh. These are not economic inequalities which can be justified, therefore, on any rational criteria. For those concerned, as political thinkers and political actors have always been, with justice in society, it is injustices of this kind – the injustices in international society, that is, the most extreme and the most irrational – that must be of primary importance today.

This applies equally to the injustices, always a matter of special concern to political observers, which result from the differential ownership of property; in particular those that result from the differential inheritance of property. It was the transmission of property, and so of privilege, from generation to generation which most outraged critics of the *ancien régime* in France and the revolutionaries which they inspired; and continued to outrage revolutionaries in other countries for the next century or more. The scale of the inequality resulting from that cause within states has now been reduced: through the effect of death duties, capital transfer taxes and similar means. Between states, however, inherited wealth continues to be the fundamental factor determining the distribution of wealth and welfare worldwide. In that case it is not so much the inherited wealth of individuals as the inheritance by *states* which is crucial in its effect.

Those who are fortunate enough to be born into wealthy societies acquire not only the economic assets enjoyed by their own immediate family, but those of their country as a whole: a vast infrastructure of educational facilities, welfare services, communications networks, public buildings and amenities, in addition to the state's general economic assets and potential, which are not available to those born within the frontiers of poorer states. The extent to which each individual can benefit from assets of this kind – can enjoy a good education, good social services, a good cultural life – therefore depends on where he is born. If the enjoyment of differential property rights through the process of inheritance is unjust, as many have argued for years, differential inheritance of this kind is equally so today. And since the consciousness of inequalities of that kind is now as great in world society as the consciousness of them in individual societies was two hundred years ago, it is inequalities of the former kind which have become the most politically significant in the modern world. Many of the most important inequalities among individuals today, therefore, derive from inequalities between the states to which they belong.

The inequalities which exist among states can, of course, as much as those which exist among individuals, be justified or at least explained. It may, for example, be held that the poverty of states which are at a low level of development results from the folly of their rulers in pursuing inappropriate economic policies. It may be held that they have brought poverty on their own people by following the prescriptions of ideology rather than of economic rationality, by the development of state-centred and state-controlled economies, rather than by relying on the guidance of markets and the ultimate sovereignty of the consumer. Or it may be believed that it results from the error of excessive protectionism, the nurturing of industry at the expense of agriculture, the subsidization of food prices at the expense of food producers, or the pursuit of an illusory "self-reliance". Or it may be put down simply to the fecklessness and inefficiency of the governments or populations of the countries concerned.

Such explanations are especially appealing to the inhabitants of rich countries since they appear to justify their own advantages. But, as in the case of inequalities among individuals, alternative explanations can be found. The cause of backwardness may be seen not in any fault on the part of the people or governments of countries concerned but on those of *other* countries. It may be felt that it is not their own pursuit of protectionism, but the protectionism of other countries, in particular the industrialized countries, depriving them of markets for their products which are vital to their development, which is mainly responsible for their difficulties. Or it may be said that it is not the subsidization of agricultural products that occurs *within* these countries, but the far more massive subsidization of agriculture which occurs in the rich countries of the world, depriving them of markets of this kind too, and even making it harder for them to compete in *third* markets too, which has held back their development. Or it is not their own preoccupation with industrialization which has led them astray, but the reluctance of industrialized countries to relinquish their own industrial capacity, even in areas, such as textiles and other simple manufacturers, where they are no longer in a position to compete effectively, which has made them poor. Or their poverty results from the imperialism of European states in by-gone days which held back their development and allowed their native crafts and industries to be swamped by cheap imports from abroad. Or it results from the neo-imperialism of multinational corporations today which, by transfer pricing and selective investment, exploit the economies of developing countries to their own advantage.

Which kind of explanation is believed will depend, as with the explanations about inequalities among individuals, not so much on rational judgements as on political preconceptions. Both types of argument are likely to be as unconvincing to their opponents as they are self-evident to their supporters. It is not impossible that all the arguments contain some smattering of the truth and none the whole of it. The poverty of many third-world countries today may result in part from the policies of their own governments in recent years; and in part from those pursued by Western countries, both now and in the distant past. What is significant, however, is not so much what explanations are put forward for the inequalities which exist; nor even which are correct. It is the fact that inequalities exist and in many cases are growing greater.

This is not because the rate of growth of poor countries is everywhere lower than that of rich countries. On the contrary, on average their rate of growth is faster. But this is mainly because of the very fast rate of growth of a small group of countries, mainly in Asia: the growth rate of African countries is much *lower* than that of industrialized states (see Table 2). But it is not the overall rate of growth that is important but the growth in living standards of their population. The lower rate of growth in living standards in poor countries comes about mainly because their populations are growing, on average, much faster than the populations of rich countries. They therefore need a substantially *higher* rate of growth in national income to maintain an equal rate of growth in income a head.

At present, because of differences in population growth, average income *a head*, already ten times greater in rich countries than in poor, continues to grow faster in the former, irrespective of overall growth rates. As the figures in Table 2 show, the advantage enjoyed

Table 2 Relative Growth Rates: Selected Groups of Countries

	1965–73	*1973–80*	*1980–5*	*1987*
Annual rates of growth in GDP:				
Industrial countries	4·5	2·8	2·4	2·9
Developing countries	6·5	5·4	3·2	3·9
Middle income	7·0	5·7	1·6	3·2
Low income	5·5	4·6	7·4	5·3
Growth of income a head:			*1980–7*	*Projected 1987–95*
Industrial countries	3·6	2·1	1·9	1·8–2·6
Developing countries	3·9	3·2	1·8	2·2–3·6
Sub-Saharan Africa	3·8	0·5	−2·9	0·0–0·7

SOURCE: World Bank Annual Report (1988) pp. 2.23.

by the inhabitants of rich countries is being reduced among middle income developing countries, especially in the newly industrialized states of the Far East. But for the poorer developing countries the gap continues to grow. Even if rates of growth per head were equal in rich countries and in poor, the gap in absolute income would continue to increase relatively rapidly. A 3 per cent increase in income a head in the US means an increase of 360 dollars per person, while the same rate of increase for Bangladesh would bring about an increase of only about 3 dollars a head. Thus the gap gets wider all the time; and the growth in income a head would have to be very much greater in poor countries, over very many years, before the gap in living standards was significantly reduced.

All of these figures relate, however, only to the *average* income a head in each country. But these averages conceal vast differences in the amounts received by individuals. Thus the current difference in the level of income of the richest decile in wealthy countries and that of the poorest decile in developing countries is even greater than that between the average incomes in the two groups; and the gap between these incomes is increasing even faster. This is the crucial political fact of contemporary international society. And it is the fact which has the greatest significance for global politics.

Within each country inequalities may be reduced by the action of individual governments, or the political activity of particular groups within those countries. But in the world as a whole the differences cannot be influenced by such means. A reduction in the most important inequalities which exist today, both among states and among individuals, cannot be brought about as a result of actions in individual states, but only by international action: action taken within world society as a whole.

THE MANAGEMENT OF THE INTERNATIONAL ECONOMY

Where inequalities among individuals in the modern world result from inequalities among states, the way of reducing them is to reduce the inequalities which exist among states.

This could only be done by finding means for the more effective management of the international economy as a whole. Within states better management systems have been developed by governments confronting the problems of national economies: for example, the problems of unemployment, inflation, depression, inadequate skills and levels of technology, geographical imbalances in rates of development, and many others. Today, all these are problems which are international rather than national, both in their causes and their effects. The depression and unemployment experienced in one country has often been exported from others; so that, it is said, when the US economy sneezes the rest of the world catches pneumonia; when the West German and Japanese economies expand too slowly, other developed countries must implore them to promote more rapid growth for the sake of the world economy as a whole. The inflation which is experienced in one country has often been created elsewhere: increases which the producer countries bring about in oil or other commodity prices affect every economy in the world, a rise in the price of capital goods and other manufactures in the West has inflationary effects for all developing countries, and so on. The rates of interest set in New York and London automatically determine the rates of interest all over the world. The protectionism of one country has a direct impact on the trade of many others. In an increasingly international economy economic problems are themselves international, and can only be resolved by international measures.

But the kinds of methods adopted in confronting these problems will affect different states and different individuals unequally. They are thus central to global politics. Just as, within states, the central issues of political controversy today often concern the choice of economic measures: those necessary to deal with domestic inflation (monetary or fiscal measures, price controls or wage controls, measures to influence demand or measures to influence supply), or to deal with unemployment (more public expenditure or less taxation, less regulation for the employer or better training for the employee, more assistance for ailing industries or better welfare for dismissed employees), so today the economic measures taken *internationally*, to deal with inflation, recession or instabilities in exchange-rates and interest-rates, become matters of acute political controversy internationally. Whether these are dealt with by international demand management or international supply side policy, by trade regulation or trade restriction, by more assistance to developing countries or stricter control of the policies that those countries pursue, by measures which demand sacrifices primarily from rich countries (or rich people) – such as more aid and easier credit – or by poor countries (or poor people) – such as more repayments and higher conditionality – these are the central economic issues of the day. The choices which are made internationally on those questions are often more important today, both for governments and their peoples, than those which are made by any individual national governments, including their own. They thus become the central issues of political as well as economic controversy.

One reason for controversy is the way in which decisions are reached. At present, in so far as international decisions are reached on these matters at all, they are reached by oligarchic bodies which represent only a few governments of the richest states: at meetings of the Group of Seven, at the regular economic "summits", and the meetings of the OECD. The decisions which are reached at those meetings are of profound importance to many other governments, rich and poor, which are not represented there. But they are of concern also to many individuals in all states, who are equally unrepresented. As the latter become more and more aware of the importance of the decisions reached by the former, they will become more concerned and anxious to influence their outcome. Those decisions, therefore, will become more and more the subject of worldwide political action.

At present such controversies arise mainly between states. The economic power of a state depends on its control over economic resources and economic events. A rich state, whatever resources may exist within its own territory, can procure the further resources which it needs from the outside world, while a poor one usually cannot. A rich state can purchase the skills and expertise of scientists, engineers and industrial managers. It can attract investment funds. It disposes of a much higher proportion of international trade, and it can direct that portion where it thinks fit. And because it is better represented, directly or indirectly, in the international bodies which have the greatest influence on world economic affairs, it is better able to control events within the international economy generally than can poorer countries. Finally, the rich state is often a creditor, and can therefore determine, either directly or through financial institutions, what action must be taken by its debtors. Most poor states, besides being dependent on others for credit, investment, trading opportunities, technology and managerial skills, are debtors, and therefore deeply dependent on their creditors.

National income is therefore usually a rough measure of the economic power of a state. A country such as Japan, for example, although militarily weak, and dependent on imports for its supplies of energy and many raw materials, exercises substantial economic power because of its high level of industrial development and consequent high income: this is shown most dramatically in Japan's ability today to exercise a substantial influence on the financial markets of other countries, even the most developed. Against this, most African countries, even large ones such as Nigeria, exercise very little economic power, and are dependent on others for their supplies of investment, capital goods, food, managerial expertise and technical skills, as well as overseas markets. To a considerable extent the economic destiny of such a country is not in its own hands but that of others. It is in an essentially dependent situation, reliant on economic decisions which are reached in other states.

Poor states today are increasingly conscious of this dependence. And the attempt to reduce it is therefore likely to be a major concern of the global politics of the future.

THE REDUCTION OF INEQUALITIES AMONG STATES

There are a number of measures which are used within states to redress inequalities in economic power. Taxation is levied on a progressive basis, reducing disposable income among the better off more than among the less privileged sections of society. Welfare services, financed in this way, are established, which provide benefits especially for those on lower incomes: since the revenue for these comes mainly from the rich and the benefits go mainly to the poor, considerable redistribution results. Finally, public services are developed and resources brought under public ownership and run for the benefit of all, a measure also intended to benefit the less well off: while the assets have often been acquired from wealthy private owners, the benefits (if any) have accrued to consumers and users of the services generally, so redressing the balance to the advantage of the latter.

Within international society each of these methods of redistribution is already used to a limited extent. Contributions to international organizations are usually levied from governments, as are taxes from individuals, on a progressive basis, so that rich countries pay more and poor countries pay less. But though some such system operates in nearly all international organizations, the total amounts involved are so small that they bring about only an insignificant transfer of resources, and then mainly from government to government rather than direct to individuals. Secondly, international agencies, financed on that basis, provide welfare services, for example, in the field of health, education, labour protection, industrial and agricultural development and a number of others: services provided to all states, but predominantly to the less privileged members of the international community. But here too the benefits so provided are relatively marginal, and again do not necessarily benefit the poorest sections of the *population* in the receiving countries. Finally, public ownership of a kind may take place at the international level – for example, through the establishment of international control over the resources of the international seabed or Antarctica – and here too the revenues obtained may be distributed in a way which predominantly benefits poorer countries (as is explicitly provided in the international treaty governing the exploitation of the seabed, and in proposals put forward for Antarctica). But here too the benefits transferred will be minimal for the foreseeable future. The resources distributed in all three ways, though they may increase marginally over future years, will remain trivial in relation to the vast inequalities which at present exist in world society between states at different levels of economic development.

In any case it is unlikely that reductions in the imbalances in economic power among states will come about as a result of decisions reached within world economic institutions. Within states, it is true, governments, through deliberate decisions on fiscal and welfare policies, may reduce the domination of the economically powerful and increase the potentialities of the economically weak. In international society, on the other hand, imbalances in economic power are if anything enhanced rather than redressed by international institutions. The most important bodies – such as the World Bank and the IMF – are dominated, under their constitutions, by the representatives of rich countries. Voting power in them depends on financial contributions, which in turn depend on economic strength. Influence within them is by definition concentrated among the wealthier countries. Thus though developing countries today represent four-fifths of the membership of those bodies, and a still larger proportion of the populations represented, they control only 30 per cent of the votes in them. Western industrialized countries, though they represent only a fifth of the membership and a smaller proportion of populations represented, control 60 per cent of the voting power. Even if, as is now possible, the Soviet Union and her partners were to join these institutions, the proportions would not be radically affected. In this sense too, therefore, economic power is overwhelmingly in the hands of the richest states.

Rich countries have more direct means of controlling economic events. They exercise a dominant influence on world trade. This is largely automatic. They control a vastly greater volume of trade in their own hands. They can by their decisions on exports, imports, trade credit and trade debts, directly determine the commercial fortunes of poorer countries, which can do little in return to affect theirs. Even if Bangladesh were to close its market altogether to the exports of one or more industrialized countries, the latter would be barely affected. But a closing by only one or two rich countries of their markets could have a catastrophic effect on many developing states. In fact poor countries are doubly dependent. They not only desperately need outlets for their own exports which must be found mainly in rich countries. They are also deeply dependent on imports from rich countries; while the latter depend on them only for a few raw materials, concentrated in a very few countries. These differences are particularly evident in the field of agricultural trade. By large-scale subsidization and protection of their farmers rich countries act to deprive the producers in poor countries of many markets which under free competition they might expect to enjoy. Poor countries can have no such influence on the markets available to farmers in rich countries, nor on the prices they can get for their products. A profound imbalance in relative economic power therefore results.

The imbalance in the financial field is equally obvious. Because of their trading difficulties poor countries are acutely dependent on financial assistance to overcome their balance of payment problems. To finance their deficits they desperately require foreign exchange. They are obliged to seek this in the form of loans, credits and new investment which they secure mainly from governments and financial institutions in wealthier states. The latter, therefore, have a potential stranglehold on their economies. It is true, as is frequently pointed out, that debtors themselves enjoy substantial leverage in their dealings with their creditors: since the latter, if they are to be sure of securing any returns on their investment, have little choice but to consider proposals for deferred repayments. But this dependence cannot be compared with that of the debtor, who knows that if he defaults on the loan he will forfeit all chance of further assistance in the future. For this reason, the debtors are obliged to take some account of the conditions which the creditors demand. The so-called "policy dialogue" which continually takes place between lenders and borrowers takes place therefore on highly unequal terms. And, as the record of these discussions over the past decade demonstrates in practice most poor countries have little option but to accept the policy prescriptions that are dictated to them by the IMF or consortia of donors.

This inequality in bargaining power is reinforced by the huge imbalance in the investment resources available to rich countries and to poor. This is the inevitable result of differences in the capital base available in each type of country. The industrial and financial resources accumulated in rich countries over a century and a half of development provide them with a large income which can be used for new investment. The average income of their population is such that even a moderate level of savings will yield substantial resources that can be used for further development in the future. That investment is made not only in productive facilities but in knowledge, skills and continuing technological progress. The assets made available in this way are far greater than can be secured through a similar rate of accumulation from the scanty resources available in poor countries. The imbalance could be redressed only if there were a substantial net flow of resources over a considerable period from rich countries to poor. But today, with the payment of earlier debts which takes place, the net flow of resources is, if anything, the other way. For a few years some flow towards developing countries still occurred, through direct investment, bank lending, and government-to-government aid programmes. But each of these flows has declined, for different reasons, in the last few years. The huge debts which poor countries have incurred has undermined the willingness of private institutions in the developed world to invest further, and of governments to add to their previous loans and aid programmes. This decline in the availability of capital resources reduces their ability to advance from declining areas of production to new and expanding ones; from simple manufacture to information technology, for example, or from agriculture to industry and the service sectors. Inequalities in the situation of the two types of country and in the resources available to them, therefore continue to increase inexorably.

More fundamental than these, perhaps, are the inequalities in educational and technical levels. Here too, for more than a century an accumulation of knowledge and skills has been taking place within the rich countries, which has continually increased their capacity for technological progress. That process has barely begun in most poor countries. This is a gap that will take very many years to bridge. Though it will not necessarily be maintained indefinitely (it was overcome by Japan, though it took her a century to do so), it will certainly not easily be narrowed. For the technological development which has already occurred provides the base for further technological development in the future so that when poor countries have reached the stage of development now reached by rich countries they may still be as far behind as they were before. And the gap which occurs in this field is one which contributes to inequalities in many other areas, including most of those which determine economic development.

For the past thirty years the more disadvantaged countries of the world have been seeking to reduce some of these inequalities among states. Apart from seeking to increase their own rates of growth through their own efforts, they have worked within international bodies to restructure the world economy to their own advantage. For a time they called for the establishment of a "new international economic order" which would operate in a way that is less disadvantageous to them than the existing economic system: in which they could secure, for example, better trading opportunities, lower interest rates, better terms of repayment of debt, greater transfer of technology and more aid on more favourable terms. Above all they have demanded a stronger voice within the international institutions where such questions are decided.

The current international economic system cannot, however, easily be altered except with the consent of the richer countries. The changes demanded could come about only as a result of changes of policy by those countries themselves, or by decisions of international organizations (such as the IMF and the World Bank) which they control. There is no reason to expect either to occur. In the eyes of the rich countries the existing economic system works perfectly well. Any change in that system would, in their eyes, be directly contrary to their national interests. In consequence they have been willing to accept only those changes – the granting of loans on softer terms, the cancellation or rescheduling of some debts, the creation of new "facilities" within the IMF, for example – which they believe can be introduced without significant sacrifice for themselves. On the more important questions they have not been willing to accept changes which they believe are contrary to the interests of their own people for whom they feel most responsible.

The governments of poor countries have little leverage with which to overcome those objections. They have little to offer in trading opportunities within their own markets to secure comparable concessions in turn. While the economic welfare of the rich countries for the most part depends little on any economic decisions they may make, they themselves are dependent on economic decisions taken by the rich. Nor are there any foreseeable developments likely to improve their situation. Aid is more likely to decline than increase; protectionism is more likely to increase than decline. The widespread belief in the "market" as the surest path to economic rationality and progress operates, in the international as in the national economy, to maximize opportunities for the strong and successful to flourish, while affording little chance to the weak and impoverished to better their position.

Only a different kind of international economic management, therefore, could *significantly* change the existing distribution of economic power in the world. But there appears little likelihood that the existing balance of economic power will be changed through traditional negotiations among governments. Self-interest is likely to continue, in this field as in many others, to be the main determinant of national policy. Only substantial political change, both nationally and internationally, could bring about the fundamental shift in power and wealth which the poorer countries seek. And it is about the means of securing that change that global politics will be concerned.

THE REDUCTION OF INEQUALITIES AMONG INDIVIDUALS

If poor countries find it difficult to bring about the changes in the international economy which they seek, it is still harder for poor individuals, scattered across the earth, in poor countries and rich alike, to secure such changes.

Even if there were, in time, some reduction in the disparities which exist among states, this would not necessarily be sufficient to reduce the inequalities which exist among individuals in international society. For there would still be vast differences in living standards within states, rich and poor alike: while the difference between the living standards of the rich in rich states and the poor in poor states would remain wider still. To influence disparities of that kind, a different type of political action is required.

If this were to become the aim it would no longer be sufficient to think in terms of a transfer of resources from rich countries to poor countries. Those concerned with this objective would need to demand a transfer of resources from rich individuals and groups to poor individuals and groups in international society as a whole.

In the first place this would require that, where resources are transferred from state to state, they were used for the benefit of those most in need in the receiving countries. At present the aid which is provided by rich countries is given, not direct to the population of the countries that are assisted, but to their governments. It is those governments which decide the purposes for which the aid is used, and so the groups who will mainly benefit from it. If the receiving government is anxious to benefit the prosperous classes from which its own political support may come, rather than the mass of the deprived; if it is concerned to assist the politically vocal urban proletariat more than the more submissive rural peasantry; if it is determined to bring about rapid "industrialization" rather than broadly-based development affecting the population as a whole, then the transfer of resources may do nothing to reduce inequalities: it may even widen them. Only if the agencies responsible were to adopt strategies specifically designed to bring benefit to those most in need would a significant redistribution take place. The aim would be to increase productive potential rather than simple relief of poverty; but it would raise the productive potential of those, such as the rural peasantry, who were most in need of help (and whose productivity could often be most rapidly improved). This is a strategy which has been adopted by one or two international agencies (notably the International Fund for Agricultural Development) and by one or two donor governments (such as Sweden). But it has not been the most common practice among providers of assistance, whether national or international.

Secondly, if the aim were redistribution within states as well as between them, international organizations would be urged to favour trade policies calculated to bring benefits especially to the poorer sections of the population of the country concerned. More effort would then be devoted – in such bodies as GATT (the General Agreement of Tariffs and Trade) and UNCTAD (the UN Conference on Trade and Development) – to overcome protectionism in agricultural products, which had adverse effects on very large numbers of the rural population in developing countries, rather than that in industrial products the avoidance of which (if conceded at all) benefits (directly at least) a much more limited number of people in poor countries while causing significant loss of employment, and even deindustrialization, in richer states. More effort would be devoted to ensuring that declines in commodity prices, which can have disastrous effect on large sections of the population in poor countries, are counter-acted by compensatory financing far more adequate than that provided at present (for example under the compensation schemes run by the IMF and the EEC): this is a far more efficient and acceptable means of assisting producers (so long as the benefits are passed on to them) than attempts to boost prices artifically through "commodity schemes". There could be agreement that, when quantitative restrictions are imposed, substantially larger quotas were offered to the "least developed countries": the 40 or so countries with the lowest income a head. And more assistance might be given to the activities of development agencies (such as Traidcraft and OXFAM) which specialize in buying handicrafts and other products from the rural poor in developing countries.

International credit policies too could be more explicitly designed to help, especially, those in greatest need. Thus the "conditionality" applied by the IMF, and by creditor countries generally, could be geared not only to the adoption of more economically rational policies, but to a commitment to policies aiming at a better distribution of income. The kind of policies demanded at present, such as the abandonment of excessive subsidization and of vast para-statal economic enterprises, would need to be matched by policies intended to assist the most disadvantaged sections of the population. The demand for policies to raise agricultural prices for rural producers might need to be matched by policies designed to improve the lot of urban consumers. The policy dialogue, which it is generally agreed is required between aid-donors and aid-recipients, would be designed not only to ensure the abandonment of economically inefficient policies but the adoption of socially beneficial ones. The conditionality demanded at present which leads to food riots and the overthrow of governments, fails, because it places too great a burden on the mass of ordinary people to procure the results the policy was intended to achieve; and in many cases the political problems created have caused governments to abandon the commitments previously made, for example to the IMF. Only if populations generally are satisfied that the policies demanded are in the long-term interests of their country and themselves individually would they willingly accept the prescription laid down. Only if they are seen to take special account of the needs of the most disadvantaged sections of the population, therefore, are they likely to be successful. It is not so much, therefore, the total abandonment of conditionality which is necessary, as it is sometimes suggested, as the adoption of a new *type* of conditionality, having socially desirable as well as economically beneficial effects.

Other types of policy, both national and international, could be demanded to affect the distribution of wealth and income within states. Programmes in the field of educational assistance (both those of international bodies such as UNESCO and those of governments) can be designed to bring about a wider distribution of skills and aptitudes; in other words, to benefit not only poor countries generally but poor people within poor countries. Assistance for irrigation works can be of a kind which bring benefits to poor peasants rather than wealthy landlords: small-scale pumps and local irrigation schemes, rather than large-scale hydro-electric works which may uproot many local inhabitants. Technical assistance can be concentrated on support for rural extension schemes, raising the productivity of agricultural producers in the countryside, rather than providing skills for industrial workers in the cities. Medical assistance can be designed to ensure adequate primary health care in the villages, rather than ultra-modern large-scale hospitals in the cities. Help to landless peasants in organizing themselves to protect their own interests and acquire a better return for their labour may be given precedence over helping the formation of western-style trade union movements.

The same aims can be promoted through the choice of *projects* to be assisted. Different types of schemes provide help for different groups of people, so that by choosing a particular project a donor, whether it is an international body, a national government or a voluntary agency, in effect chooses which type of group it wishes to help. A decision to support a rural health project (rather than supplying equipment for a modern steel mill) is a decision to help a large number of rural poor rather than a small number of urban workers. A decision to provide a better water supply for urban shanty towns, rather than to provide expensive equipment for a new factory, is a decision to help some of the most deprived sections of a country's population, rather than to help a major industrialist to become marginally more efficient (and the country to reduce a tiny fraction of its imports).

The choice of the organizations through which assistance is channelled can have a similar effect. A decision to work through voluntary agencies or local community organizations, rather than through the government of the country concerned or corrupt local officials, may ensure that aid reaches a different group of people, and helps them more directly and more effectively, than would otherwise be the case. Aid that is provided through a non-governmental organization known to be committed to helping the poorest groups in society (such as OXFAM) may be more likely to bring help to those most in need than a decision to work only through official channels. The earmarking of assistance for particular regions or city districts which are the most deprived and have most poor inhabitants will ensure that the redistributive effect of the aid is maximized. Decisions concerning the choice of international organizations for channelling aid may have a similar effect. If more money is allocated to UNICEF and less to the UN Industrial Development Organization, more to the International Fund for Agricultural Development and less to the International Civil Aviation Organization, there will be a change not only in the purposes for which it is used but in those who are assisted.

At present public opinion within the donor countries makes little effort to influence choices of this kind. Usually it has no idea how the amounts of money given by their own governments in development assistance is spent. Yet the decisions made on that question can have a vital effect in determining the distribution of the benefits provided. Only if groups and individuals, in both donor and receiving countries, become more informed about such questions, will they be able to influence the decisions reached about the way such assistance is employed.

At the very least there should be, in a global political system, far more discussion about such issues. If inequalities between those living in different states rather than those living in the same one have become the most important in the modern world, there should be, in rich countries and poor alike, far more debate than there is today about the best means of remedying the inequalities. Far more than today, direct links may come to be established between disadvantaged groups in different states and different types of state. These may then become the instruments for a more deliberate and well-organized effort to influence decisions on such matters than is normally made today. Such movements could affect not only decisions about assistance policies and the relief of debt, but concerning the management of the international economy generally. Management of that kind, affecting the world economy as a whole, can have a far greater effect on the economic well-being of individuals in all parts of the world than the decisions which are reached individually by the governments of each such state. Eventually it may begin to be recognized that it is influence on these decisions which is most significant politically. For it is those decisions, it will be understood, which will have the greatest effect on the distribution of wealth and welfare within international society as a whole.

7 The Functional Institutions of World Society

THE ROLE OF INSTITUTIONS

All those concerned with politics have been concerned with the character of political institutions.[1] For they have recognized that these play a decisive role in determining the political outcomes – the distribution of benefits – in any political system.

Political theorists have analysed institutions within states according to the functions they perform. They have discussed the differing functions performed by legislature, executive and judicature, and the degree to which these should be made independent of each other. They have considered electoral systems, parliamentary procedures and the administration of justice. And they have been concerned to compare the relative effectiveness of different institutional arrangements in achieving such purposes as government by consent, the maintenance of law and order, the harmonization of conflicting interests, efficient decision-making, or the "authoritative allocation of values".

Political actors too have recognized the central importance of institutions. So political reformers in England and other countries campaigned above all for a strengthening of the powers of parliament and an extension of the franchise. Revolutionaries in France and other states demanded above all a reform of the institutions dispensing justice and an end to the sale of administrative offices. Socialists in Germany and elsewhere called for the transformation of economic institutions to bring about the social justice they demanded. Everywhere the reform of institutions was seen as the essential condition for the reform of society as a whole.

The institutions which have been most discussed by political theorists, and built up by political activists, have been state institutions. These were the institutions on which the welfare of the

1. The author is grateful to the editor of *International Affairs* for permission to make use in this chapter of material that first appeared in that journal.

citizen seemed most to depend. But those institutions have become, for reasons we have examined earlier, increasingly incapable of performing effectively the tasks demanded of them. However efficiently they may work at the local level, they are no longer able to respond to the needs which make themselves felt most acutely in modern world society. A system of national decision-making, however efficiently it operates, and whatever consent it may secure from the local citizenry, is no longer adequate when a large proportion of the problems confronted derive from outside the state. Political institutions that satisfactorily resolve conflicts of interest within each state are irrelevant when the most important conflicts of interest occur *between* separate states, or between groups and individuals in different states. Legal institutions which effectively accomplish the administration of justice within states are inadequate in a world where the most manifest injustices exist between states. The maintenance of law and order within states, however efficiently it is undertaken, becomes of less significance when criminal organizations, drug traffic, terrorist movements, the hi-hacking or aircraft, as well as the organized violence of governments, operate between states rather than within them. For this reason what matters most to the welfare of citizens is no longer the improvement of the institutions which exist at the national level but improvement of those which operate globally: that is, of *international* institutions. Yet so far, much less attention has been devoted to the way these operate.

Such institutions have existed for centuries. Some have been designed to perform functions not unlike those performed within national states. The settlement of disputes has been undertaken by procedures for arbitration, mediation and good offices, supplemented in recent years by a Permanent Court of Arbitration, the International Court of Justice and regional courts (for example in Europe and Latin America). Political communication among states, and the discussion of common problems, has been undertaken by diplomatic machinery, intergovernmental conferences, summit meetings among statesmen and, more recently, various types of international organization. Embryonic machinery for the maintenance of law and order has been established: in the Concert of Europe, the League of Nations, and latterly by the United Nations. Various functional tasks have been performed on an international basis: in the field of health, education, agriculture, labour protection, air and sea communication, posts and telegraphs, by specialized agencies established for those purposes.

There have been severe limitations in the capacity of these

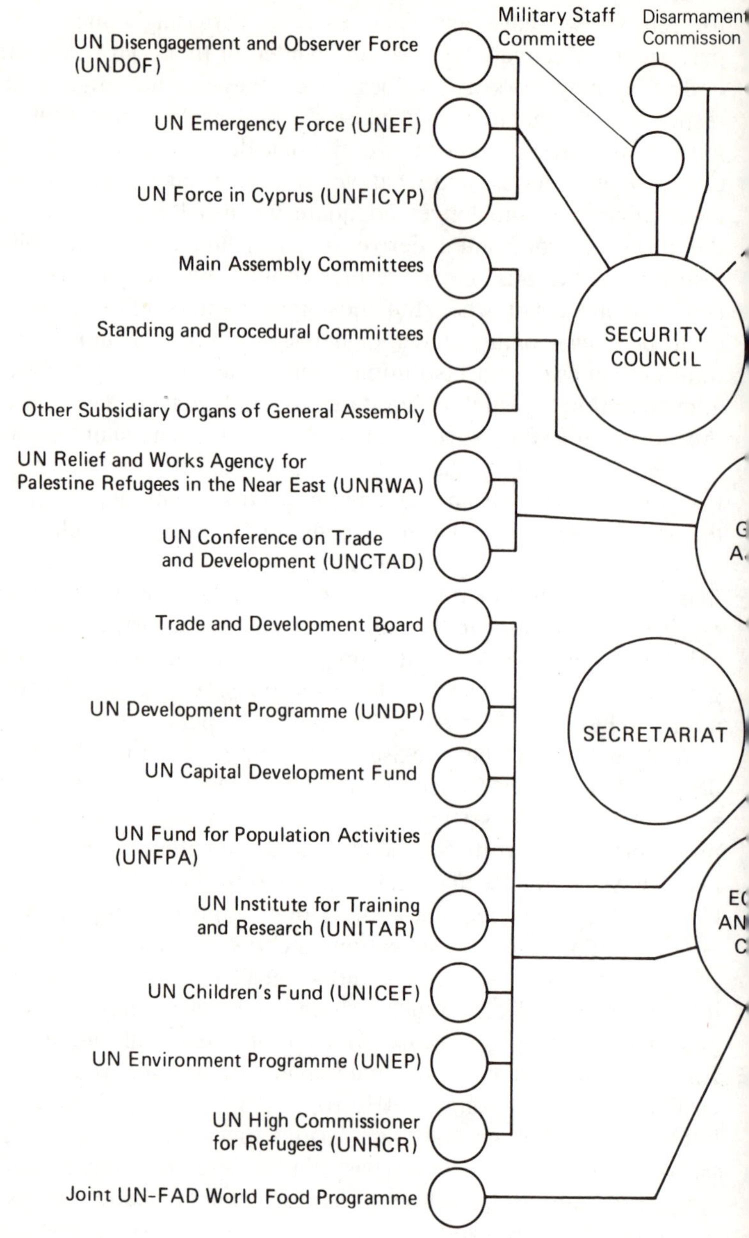

Figure 1 Structure of the United Nations and the agencies

THE SPECIALIZED AGENCIES, IAEA, AND GATT

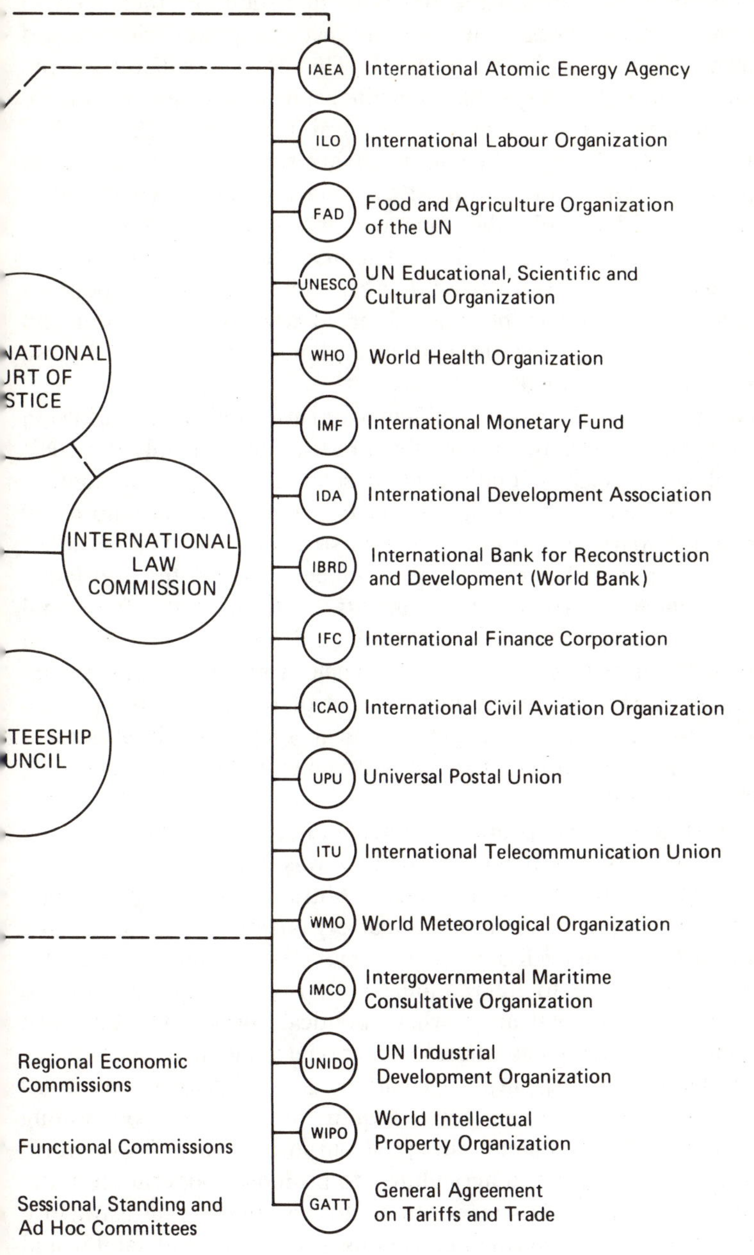

organizations to perform the functions demanded of them. Those limitations derive principally from the fact that power within world society has remained decentralized. The power available to the members of that society – the individual states – has remained large in relation to that available to the central institutions. The result is that the latter have, unlike national institutions, been unable to impose their will; and so in most cases have remained incapable of performing adequately the functions which contemporary international society requires of them. The inadequacies of this structure have become widely recognized. Increasingly, therefore, the political action that is relevant becomes directed towards the reform and remodelling of these world-wide institutions, rather than of those that exist at the national level.

One reason for the inadequacies in world institutions is the diffusion of authority. International functional institutions – mainly the UN's specialized agencies – operate at present as virtually autonomous entities. Within national states functional agencies are normally component parts of the governmental structure. They come under the direct political control of governments and of the legislative bodies which control the governments. Reform of the functional agencies is therefore undertaken through decisions of these central bodies. In international society the agencies which perform the main functional tasks are largely independent of the central body – the United Nations – seen as the main political organ within international society. Reform can therefore be undertaken only within each such body separately.

This degree of independence is deliberate. At the time when the United Nations was being founded, it was held by exponents of "functionalist" theory, such as David Mitrany, that the main hope for the development of international organizations was not in the political field, where disagreements among states were most acute, and the resistance to international authority was greatest, but in the various functional areas where political cooperation was then beginning to develop and where international antagonisms were likely to be least. For this purpose separate, non-political organizations were required. If nations could acquire the habit of cooperating within these for commonly accepted purposes – to improve world health, to develop world agriculture, to promote cooperation in the field of education and science, to create an effective infrastructure for world posts and telecommunications, and so on – that habit would eventually spill over into the political arena. So a "working peace system" would be established, and a more harmonious international order would slowly come into being.[2]

There were always weaknesses in this theory. Was it true that the new specialized agencies to perform these various practical tasks would be free of political disputes? Even if cooperation in these functional areas could be effectively established, would there be a "spill-over" into the more contentious political arena? Was it not possible that a movement in the opposite direction might take place: that violent political and ideological conflicts, expressed first in political bodies, would eventually also spill over into the specialized agencies and would damage the effort to establish effective cooperative arrangements there?

Despite doubts of this kind, many people probably felt when the UN family was established that the system of specialized agencies, now more numerous than before and integrated more closely within the UN framework, was one of the most hopeful features of the post-war international scene. And today it would still be widely judged that the development of these activities has been the most positive achievement of the UN system.

In the field of peace and security the performance of the United Nations is viewed by many with disappointment. The United Nations has appeared to be able to do little to prevent wars from erupting; still less to bring them to an end after they have broken out. Expenditure on armaments is higher than ever before in peace time, among poor and weak countries as much as among the most powerful. The only area of UN activity which has, to some extent, prospered and grown is that undertaken by the specialized agencies and other functional bodies within the system, which operate today on a far bigger scale than most people originally envisaged.

This expansion can be measured partly simply in terms of the growth of the budgets of the various agencies concerned. The regular budgets of the specialized agencies themselves, for example, grew from about $300 million in 1970 and over $1,000 million in the early eighties. Expenditure over and above that, financed by the United Nations Development Programme (UNDP) and other voluntary funds (including spending within the United Nations itself), has grown even faster, from $8 million in 1950, to $150 million in 1960, $400 million in 1970 and around $2,000 million in the early eighties. The number of agencies has grown steadily, from five or so when the

2. David Mitrany, *A Working Peace System* (London, 1943).

Second World War ended to 15 today. The number of employees of the system has grown from a few thousand to over 50,000.

More significantly, the range of problems tackled by the UN family has increased steadily during this period. Substantial programmes are now undertaken in such fields as the environment, the care of refugees, population, disaster relief, and many others, scarcely thought of when the United Nations began. The development assistance side of each agency's work has multiplied many times: all are now involved, on a larger scale than ever, in field work within developing countries all over the world. Even the United Nations itself has become increasingly engaged in such practical work on the ground, as well as organizing a huge variety of discussions, including large-scale international conferences, which have focused world attention in turn on such matters as the environment, population, women, habitation and science and technology.

The fact that there has been so much activity of this kind is no guarantee that it has been effective: that is "functional". There is fairly general agreement that many of the agencies are overmanned, bureaucratic and sometimes inefficient. They have certainly not escaped political controversy, sometimes of a petty and irrelevant kind. And they inevitably suffer problems inherent in multinational, multilingual organizations, with staffs from widely varying cultural and political backgrounds, and ultimately run by assemblies of 150-odd nations, each with different conceptions of the primary purposes of the organization in question. These are partly difficulties that all international bodies must encounter. But for the global political system the question arises: could the tasks be better performed than they are now?

POLITICAL CONFLICT AS A CONSTRAINT ON EFFECTIVENESS

Let us first look at the main problems that have been encountered by these various organizations since their foundation. This may help us to reach some judgements about the prospects for their future development.

First, the idea that organizations with limited functional objectives would be free of political conflict quickly proved itself unfounded. Delegates from individual groups frequently raise within them extraneous political issues which are only barely related to the main purposes of the organization concerned. Throughout their history, but especially during the first decade or two of their existence, East–West conflicts have frequently erupted within them. At the beginning of the 1950s, at the height of the cold war, the Soviet Union left most of the agencies altogether for two or three years. In the 1970s the US left the International Labour Organization (ILO) also largely for political reasons.

Secondly there have been, even more often, conflicts of a North–South character (which quite often push the Soviet Union and the United States into the same camp). The most widespread and the most fundamental of these disputes has concerned the level of expenditure to be undertaken by each agency. Because a substantial proportion of expenditure in all of them in recent years has been for development-related purposes, bringing special benefits to poor countries, and because a major part of the revenues is provided by rich countries, it is inevitable that the former are more enthusiastic supporters of large-scale programmes than the latter. Every year or two (according to the periodicity of the budget cycle) there takes place a major battle within each agency on this question, concerning not the fact of budgetary increase but the pace. Usually a compromise is reached which used to be closer to the view of the developing countries than that of the rich states (since the former have the votes and the latter no veto on this question). The richer Western countries confer together regularly about these problems, and usually seek to contain budget increases, but have only limited power (short of leaving the organizations altogether) to prevent them. They can only hope to persuade the executive heads and the rest of the membership of the need to show moderation. The Western powers have sometimes acted in concert with the Soviet Union on such matters, especially within the UN itself, in making private representations to the senior officials. By these means they have in recent years succeeded in restraining the growth of the budgets in real terms. This is a battle that will inevitably continue because it relates to one of the most fundamental questions in any political system: the volume of redistribution that will be undertaken through the public spending system. The problem is inherent in the structure of the agencies and there is no built-in formula for resolving it.

Another type of political conflict which has afflicted these organizations concerns the bilateral issues between individual members which are so often injected into their proceedings. The most persistent and the most acute is the Arab–Israeli dispute, which has been expressed, in one form or another, in almost all the agencies, and has caused serious crises in one or two, for example the UN Educational, Scientific and Cultural Organization (UNESCO) and the ILO. Quite often a grievance of this kind is of such overriding and passionate concern to one or more member states that they cannot resist the temptation to bring it to the surface at every available opportunity. Usually such a member will have little difficulty in finding some aspect of the political problem which is related to the concern of the agency concerned: the Arabs raise Israeli excavations in east Jerusalem in UNESCO or labour practices in the occupied territories in the ILO. Whatever justification may be found under the letter of the organization's constitution for raising such questions, those who indulge in this practice will usually forfeit rather than win support by doing so (as the injection of East–West issues by either side has often done), since most members resent the intrusion of essentially irrelevant issues.

A fourth problem from which all the agencies have suffered (though it is the system as a whole which has suffered rather than the individual agencies) is the lack of an effective system of coordination. In theory the agencies belong to a common "family" or system, within which they enjoy a considerable degree of autonomy. In practice the autonomy is far more evident than the family relationship. Three of the specialized agencies were in existence before the United Nations was founded (the International Telecommunication Union, the Universal Postal Union, and the ILO) and have always resented being placed under even theoretical "coordination" by the United Nations. The newer agencies are equally strongly committed to preserving their own independence of action. A vast mechanism for coordination has been established to try to create a semblance of order among this teeming swarm of children: the Economic and Social Council (ECOSOC), which is the main intergovernmental body responsible; the Committee for Programme and Coordination (CPC), the committee established by ECOSOC for the purpose; and the Administrative Committee on Coordination (ACC), the official body composed of the executive heads under the Secretary-General's chairmanship, as well as other bodies.[3] Though this effort has succeeded in reducing

3. For a more detailed discussion of the problems of coordination within the UN family, see Douglas Williams, *The Specialised Agencies and the United Nations* (London: Hurst, 1987) pp. 177–95; and Evan Luard, *International Agencies: The Emerging Framework of Interdependence* (London: Macmillan, 1978), ch. 17.

somewhat the problems of duplication and overlapping jurisdiction which previously existed and in establishing certain common services and institutions, it has done little to create a genuinely coordinated programme for the system as a whole. Each agency for the most part goes its own sweet way and takes as little notice as possible of the various exhortations made upon it to comply with the policy decisions made elsewhere, for example in ECOSOC or in the General Assembly. (See Table 3.)

Table 3 Coordination Within the UN System

UN family	*United Nations Proper*
Economic and Social Council (ECOSOC) (54 governments): coordinates the activities of the specialized agencies through "consultation" and "recommendations".	*Economic and Social Council (ECOSOC) (54 governments): coordinates economic and social work of the United Nations.*
Administrative Committee on Coordination (ACC) (executive heads of the agencies under chairmanship of UN Secretary-General): discusses coordination of activities and avoidance of overlap.	*Committee on Programmes and Coordination (CPC) (representatives of 21 governments): examines programmes and budget within the United Nations.*
Advisory Committee on Administrative and Budgetary Questions (ACABQ) (16 financial experts, from a variety of countries): advises on administrative economies.	
Joint inspection Unit (JIU) (experts on administration): advises on administrative efficiency.	

If the functional operations of the UN family are to be made more effective, there is a need for progress in resolving all these difficulties: reductions in East–West rivalry, in North–South disputes and in extraneous political controversies, and an increase in effective UN coordination. It would, however, be wishful thinking to expect substantial progress in any of these areas. The hope of the functionalists that political controversy could be excluded from the agencies was always a somewhat forlorn one. Although it is reasonable to try to minimize the difficulties and to concentrate on the main purposes of each organization, political conflicts will continue to make themselves felt. Some of the decisions to be reached in the agencies are essentially political and it is idle to hope that politics can be generally banned. Continuing attempts to establish a more effective coordination are undoubtedly required, but the built-in tendency towards decentralization of decision-making in the system (which has merits as well as disadvantages) will not be altogether overcome.

These are only some of the more general problems of the system. If the purposes they fulfil are to be better accomplished in the next decade, it will be necessary to look more closely at the changes that will be needed to improve these bodies' effectiveness.

THE FUNCTIONS TO BE PERFORMED

What are the primary functions the agencies will be called on to exercise in the coming years?

The influx of new members in the 1960s brought strong pressures from a large part of the membership of each agency for expansion in its development activities. The rich countries have not seriously resisted this change, although they have had reservations about the scale of it. What the latter have often sought to do is to ensure that the new programmes are financed by voluntary funds rather than by the regular budget. In this way, they have felt they could retain greater control over the speed of growth. They have not entirely succeeded. A considerable part of the development assistance side of the agencies' work is today financed by voluntary funds: the UNDP or occasionally other funds. This gives the richer countries greater control over the scale of their operations. But all the agencies now also devote a part of their regular budgets to technical assistance and other development activities.

This trend will continue. In many cases assistance to less advanced countries is vital to the main purposes of the organization. The International Civil Aviation Organization (ICAO) cannot fulfil its main role of securing efficient and safe navigation facilities for aircraft throughout the world unless it helps poorer countries to improve the standards of their equipment and services, since most of the problems in this respect inevitably occur in the developing world. The World Meteorological Organization (WMO) cannot provide an efficient world weather service unless it ensures that poorer members (sometimes situated in areas that are especially crucial for information about weather patterns) have the facilities and equipment for providing the information needed. But, even where development assistance is not so *immediately* necessary for fulfilling an agency's purpose, it may still in the long run be essential in achieving its goals. If the World Health Organization (WHO) is to improve health standards all over the world, it must help to improve health standards (especially sanitation and water supply) in the poor countries of the world where they are at present most inadequate. If UNESCO is to improve world educational standards, it must assist education in the poorest countries where most help is required. And so on.

For these reasons the pressure for more assistance work by the agencies and for more funds to carry it out is certain to be maintained in the years to come. Western countries will no doubt demand efficient and economical use of the funds provided for this purpose, and there will continue to be controversy about the precise rate of growth. But, given the scale of the needs to be met, it seems likely that the development side of the agencies' activities will continue to grow. And the agencies specifically concerned with development will probably grow fastest.

The World Bank is in a different position from most of the other agencies in that, so far as its traditional hard lending is concerned, it can raise the funds it requires in the market, and is not therefore dependent on the decisions of governments for securing resources (its underlying capital base has recently been doubled to assist this). Its lending ("commitments") in recent years has risen in a spectacular fashion, having grown from about $500 million in 1960 to $2,000 million in 1970 and over $15,000 million in the late eighties. Since the calls on its funds will continue, and since its capacity to raise money in the markets remains high, this rate of growth may continue, though its normal operations may only be attractive to middle-income countries that can afford the interest charges. The Bank's soft-loans affiliate, the International Development Authority (IDA), will grow more slowly, since in this case "replenishment" does depend on the decisions of governments (and therefore of the US Congress, which has shown itself increasingly reluctant to approve such appropriations recently). But the World Bank family as a whole, the expertise of which is recognized by rich countries and poor alike, is likely to continue to play a dominant role in development work.

It seems probable that there will also be a significant strengthening of the International Monetary Fund (IMF) in the years to come. This has been called for by many in the West, as much as among developing countries. The interests of rich countries and poor in a stronger IMF are rather different, but in each case powerful. Influential figures within the developed countries increasingly think in terms of giving a stronger role to the IMF in securing "adjustment" by poor countries and in supervising debt-rescheduling agreements. The growing balance-of-payments and debt problems being experienced by developing countries have brought increasing resort to the IMF. This has already caused adjustments to the IMF system: increasing use of "facilities", rather longer-term credit, increasing regard for the supply side in the adjustments demanded. The growing caution of the international banking system and increasing indebtedness means that the IMF's role will now be magnified. This will intensify the calls, already widely made, for an easing of "conditionality" and a wider sharing of decision-making in the IMF, so that voting rights in the Executive Board are not so highly concentrated among rich countries as is the case today (the developed countries now have 60 per cent of the votes, oil-producers 10 per cent, and poor countries 30 per cent). Pressures will grow for a non-proportional increase in quotas so that voting rights are more evenly shared between rich countries and poor: the effect of this would be that neither side need feel it is being excessively dominated by the other.

In the field of trade there have been proposals for rationalization of the present untidy structure. Some would like to see the establishment of something like the old International Trade Organization (ITO) that was envisaged in the Havana Charter of 1947 but was eventually rejected by the US Congress. It seems doubtful if any such change will come about. The existing dichotomy between the General Agreement on Tariffs and Trade (GATT) and the United Nations Conference on Trade and Development (UNCTAD) – the one devoted to a series of businesslike negotiations on trade liberalization which have brought benefits mainly to the rich states, the other devoted to a collective dialogue between rich countries and poor in which the poor have the louder voice – unsatisfactory though it may seem, reflects a real need. In the former, there are down to earth negotiations for binding trade agreements; and, in the latter a much more political confrontation, in which poor countries can use the weight of their numbers to exert pressure for more radical change. A change in the structure would not alter this reality. Both kinds of body, or at least both kinds of activity, would continue to be required. Even the existing subsidiary bodies – such as the UNCTAD committees on shipping, insurance, commodities, preferences and so on – would probably need to be re-established. The most that is therefore likely to occur in practice is a further tidying-up of the remaining duplication and overlap, together with the establishment of closer links between the two bodies, perhaps under some common umbrella.

There may well be calls for new roles to be performed by UN agencies. One task for which UN action is likely to be increasingly demanded is monitoring the activities of transnational corporations (TNCs). Although the rapid growth in the share of these companies in world economic activity may have slowed somewhat, it remains phenomenal, especially in the field of banking. The concern of many developing countries at the power these companies wield, and at their ability to inhibit governmental decision-making, remains acute. So far the main role of the UN's Commission on Transnational Corporations has been essentially of a fact-finding character. But its most immediate task, as it acknowledges, is the negotiation of a set of guidelines for the activities of the corporations which will receive widespread recognition by the governments of rich states and poor alike and will also, it is to be hoped, be accepted by the corporations themselves. If it succeeds in that task, it may then have a role in supervising the way the guidelines are implemented by individual corporations. What is certain is that, given the increasing economic power of these corporations and their ability to slip between the network of the sovereignty of individual states, there will continue to be concern about their activities and calls for international measures to govern their activities.

The conclusion of the negotiations for a treaty governing the seabed could also lead to institutional changes. If the convention secures sufficient ratifications, the new International Seabed Authority will be empowered to negotiate and approve contracts for exploitation; it will help to establish an international enterprise which would itself be responsible for developing half the exploitable area; it will supervise and enforce the observance of environmental, safety and other regulations to safeguard the area: and it will formulate and administer a general depletion policy for the minerals of the region. For the first time, therefore, an international agency will be disposing of international resources – resources of very great value – and using the revenues for the benefit of mankind as a whole. The system will also, as is widely recognized, require an effective disputes procedure, since there will be ample scope for conflict both between individual nations and between nations and the authority. Whatever the details, the system will represent a wholly new development within international society: the establishment of a considerable degree of international control over resources, generally regarded as the common property of mankind, and a measure of international authority over a substantial section of the earth's surface. The way that authority is operated will become a source of great controversy in international relations.

Another functional area that is now receiving increasing international attention is that of energy. In the eyes of many it is extraordinary and anomalous that, despite the importance of energy problems within the world economy today, no international body with this responsibility yet exists. The only UN agency at present active in this field is the International Atomic Energy Agency (IAEA) but its responsibilities are highly specialized and it clearly cannot become the forum for the general discussion of energy problems. In recent years, the UNDP and the World Bank have both greatly increased their funding of energy activities, but do not organize general discussions of energy policy. The only other bodies which have been active in this field have been international interest groups, such as the Organization of Petroleum Exporting Countries (OPEC), representing the oil producers, and the International Energy Agency (IEA), representing most of the industrial consumers. There has recently been considerable discussion of what type of institution is required for this purpose. Kurt Waldheim, when UN Secretary-General, proposed a UN "energy institute" with mainly a research and fact-finding role; but as yet this proposal has not been implemented.

The main reason why no such international energy body exists at present is the implacable hostility of the oil-producing countries. They have opposed the establishment of any international organization with authority in this field, since they are fearful that such a body, whatever the formal position, would inevitably exercise an indirect influence on price negotiations. Until recently these countries, despite their obviously self-interested position, were able to exercise a remarkable degree of influence on other developing countries, whose true interest was in fact far otherwise. This position has, however, shifted a little over recent years. There is an increasing recognition that the questions of availability of energy supplies, energy saving and the development of alternative energy sources require systematic international discussion and debate. This process was begun at the 1981 UN

Conference on New and Renewable Sources of Energy held in Nairobi. It is now increasingly accepted (and demanded by rich countries) that energy must be one of the major themes of the North–South debate in the years to come.

It is possible that at some future date a new specialized agency will be established which will assume responsibility in this field, provided agreement can be reached on its precise terms of reference. More likely perhaps, in the first place, is the establishment of a "centre" within the UN Secretariat, or even a semi-autonomous body within the United Nations on the lines of UNCTAD. Such a body could still at some time in the future develop into a full-scale, autonomous specialized agency. Meanwhile the World Bank, in response to strong opposition from the Reagan administration in the United States, has suspended its attempts to set up an energy affiliate to help poor countries explore and develop their own energy sources. What is certain is that the many problems which will arise in this area, especially concerning the prospective global energy balance, will require systematic discussion on an international basis and thus an appropriate forum in which to undertake these discussions.

It is possible that a broader concern about the world's decreasing resources will be expressed within the UN system over the coming years. There is an increasing consciousness in many countries today of the threat to mankind's future that could result from the rapid and often wasteful running down of the earth's finite stock of minerals and other resources. Although this is most visible, and most widely deplored, in the case of the non-renewable fuels, such as oil, gas and uranium, the same position exists (and may be less easily remedied by alternative sources) in the case of other minerals. Effective policies for the management of these resources can only be satisfactorily devised and implemented at the international level, because the problem itself is an international one. There may therefore be demands, from the general public, from environmental bodies, and from concerned governments, for the establishment of a body which could take responsibility in this area (the existing Committee on Natural Resources established under ECOSOC, which is concerned mainly with assistance for natural resources development, is neither qualified nor inclined to do this). A new International Resources Commission, or something of the type, is required to keep the question under permanent review.

There is another "functional" need of wider importance, one that perhaps requires global management even more urgently than those discussed above: for some body that would keep under review the needs of the international economy as a whole. The lack of any body equipped to undertake this function has been widely recognized. Neither the IMF nor the World Bank is well equipped to undertake this responsibility, despite the fact that their joint annual meeting does provide the opportunity for an exchange of views between finance ministers from all over the world. On the other hand, the so-called economic summits, which are very much concerned with the problem of world economic management, are confined to the heads of state of a few advanced Western countries. So far they have taken little interest in the economic problems of the other five-sixths of the world.

One way to approach the matter would be to set up a body of experts, comparable to the present Committee on Development Planning (or, at the national level, to the Committee of Economic Advisers to the US President), whose function it would be to consider the present state of the world economy, to issue periodic reports, and to tender advice to governments and to relevant UN bodies. A more ambitious move, which might have to wait several years after the first had been accomplished, would be to organize periodic meetings under UN auspices of a small but well-balanced body of finance ministers or even heads of government in order to exchange views on policy requirements and to issue an agreed statement of recommendations. The IMF–World Bank Development Committee, composed of finance ministers, could conceivably provide the nucleus for this. The main benefit of this procedure, as in other areas of UN activity, would be not so much the "decisions" themselves, which at first will probably have only a marginal influence on governments, as its effect in establishing the habit of considering such questions on an international basis, so as to make all governments more aware of the international implications of any national policy options they may have in mind.

PROBLEMS OF GROWTH AND MANAGEMENT

Though the most important, the foregoing are not the only developments likely to affect the UN functional bodies over the coming years. There will also no doubt be a continued *expansion* in areas in which the UN family has already become involved. It seems, unhappily, only too likely, for example, that there may be a need for a further increase in the role which the United Nations plays in the care of refugees, already a vast and rapidly growing responsibility for the organization. In the past few years alone, events in South-East Asia, Afghanistan and Central America have hugely added to this work-load and it would be optimistic to assume that such crises will not continue to recur with great regularity in the coming decade. The work of the High Commissioner suffers seriously at present from the precariousness of sources of finance. Though it will no doubt continue to depend on voluntary pledges, the work of the UN High Commission for Refugees (UNHCR) would be enormously assisted if governments pledged for two or three years at a time, and for the general budget rather than for specific groups of refugees. Similarly, given the continued growth of the drug problem all over the world and the international ramifications of the drug trade, there will almost certainly be need for further intensification of the activities of the UN Fund for Drug Abuse Control and for more resources to be devoted by member governments to this work. The work of the UN Fund for Population Activities (UNFPA), likewise financed by voluntary contributions, is also likely to expand, and the UNFPA will require far larger resources than it has available today if it is to be in a position to respond effectively to the continuing crisis that high birth rates create for the poorest countries in the world. Because rapid population growth cannot easily be matched by increases in food resources, the International Fund for Agricultural Development (IFAD), which has a special responsibility for helping raise food population in the poorest countries, may also need additional resources to fulfil its tasks. These are only a few of the more obvious growth points. The demands on the system will certainly increase, and the pressure for larger budgets and programmes in all the agencies of the UN system is unlikely to decline perceptibly in the years to come.

If the growth of expenditure in all these activities is to be matched by a corresponding growth in effectiveness, however, there will be a need for a new concern to improve the administrative efficiency of each agency and of the system as a whole. So far as efficiency within each agency is concerned, probably the major need is for changes in the way staff are initially recruited. All the secretariats are inevitably under strong pressure to achieve some kind of geographical balance in the composition of their staffs. But the countries that bring this pressure are not always willing or able to offer recruits of the necessary qualifications. It will never be possible to escape the pressures for geographical balance. Organizations that claim to be international must have international staffs (and developed countries, which complain about pressures for "equitable geographical distribution", themselves bring very strong influence to bear when senior appointments in a secretariat are at issue). What can, however, be demanded is that, while the attempt is made to secure a reasonable balance, standards of entry should not be lowered.

A second requirement if greater efficiency is to be achieved is to allow greater scope and authority to the UN's Joint Inspection Unit (JIU), whose purpose it is to bring about improvements in this sphere. The Unit has over the past 25 years produced a series of first-class reports on the administrative failings of the system, both on the general problems affecting all the agencies and on defects relating to individual operations and units. A large proportion of the reports, however, have scarcely been noticed: the agencies continue to resent any criticism of their operations that emanates from outside bodies. The Advisory Committee on Administrative and Budgetary Questions (ACABQ), which has undertaken detailed examination of most of the agencies in addition to its normal budgetary scrutiny, has also been to a large extent ignored.

At root, the difficulty lies in the bureaucratic resistance to change that is inevitably encountered in large-scale organizations. What is probably required is the establishment *within* each agency of some unit, preferably intergovernmental in character, to take responsibility for considering all such matters, including JIU reports, and for recommending action on them. For this, as for everything else within international organizations, the fundamental responsibility lies with member governments. If enough of them consistently devote sufficient attention to the problem, clamour loud enough for reform and mobilize the right kind of third-world support, something will be done. And if the Geneva Group of developed countries were to devote itself more systematically to trying to bring about changes of this kind, instead of dedicating itself to systematic budget-cutting, it would be more likely to achieve something useful.

Finally, and quite as important as either of these tasks, if the UN system is to be made more responsive, a much more effective system of coordination must be established. There is no subject that has been so much discussed and disputed within the UN system. From the very first years of its existence the question has caused problems. Innumerable institutional changes have been made in an attempt to improve the situation. A succession of new coordinating bodies has been set up. The root of the problem, however, lies in the highly autonomous role given to the specialized agencies at the time when the system was established. Though that decision has often been criticized, mainly because of the very problem of divided authority which it has produced, it is not the case that a more centralized system would necessarily have worked better. It might indeed have merely produced a still larger and more unwieldy bureaucracy, and more uncertain lines of command than exist today. The agencies are in general performing relatively specialized tasks in specialized fields. These would not always be performed better if they had even more eyes peering over their shoulders or more layers of supervision placed above them.

A more feasible alternative to the present structure might have been one in which the *funds* for each agency came from a single source, or at least a single budgetary decision, but, once granted, could be spent by the agencies as they chose. In that case a minimal but essential power of coordination – the power of the purse, the ability of a central body to determine the volume of *total* spending as well as the balance *between* agencies – could have been combined with a substantial executive independence for each subsidiary body. It is unlikely, however, that a change of this magnitude could be implemented now. An alternative reform is required.

It is arguable that coordination between the different parts of the system as a whole, though clearly a problem, is a less acute one than coordination within the United Nations itself, with its proliferation of Assembly committees, subsidiary bodies, "programmes" and "centres" (some of them financed, wholly or in part, from voluntary funds) which virtually decide their own programmes and levels of expenditure. In theory, the Assembly is not supposed to vote on a new programme without an indication of the financial implications and, if possible, the comments of the ACABQ. But in practice, once an individual Assembly Committee has reached a decision to expand or add a programme, there is little disposition among the delegations to query that decision. The secretariat must then proceed to make provision for it in the forthcoming budget, new staff must be hired, new accommodation provided, new equipment acquired. So a programme is launched which then acquires a momentum of its own and may continue indefinitely. In practice, once a programme has been started, a vested interest in its continuation grows up and it becomes difficult to halt. Thus new programmes are added piecemeal at each General Assembly on the recommendation of one or another subsidiary committee, with little regard for what has been done before or what is being done elsewhere in one of the other agencies. The first need, therefore, is for a reform of the Assembly's budgetary procedure. What is essential is that the opportunity is provided, as is not the case today, for an overall view to be taken, so that at some stage – before, not after, the essential programme-creating decision is reached – a genuine assessment is made of the resources available, the needs to be met, and the requirement for the programme to be endorsed.

Coordination within the UN family as a whole is a wider and more difficult problem. The avoidance of overlap and duplication is gradually being achieved, through the operation of the ACC and its subordinate bodies, though new problems constantly recur. Since it is very difficult to induce any agency to withdraw altogether from a programme on which it has embarked, this process normally must be confined to ensuring that each agency tackles only that aspect of the disputed area (say water resources, agricultural education, community development) which is strictly relevant to its own concerns. Sometimes a new programme covering the field in question can be used to provide coordination: so the UN Environment Programme (UNEP) is able (in theory at least) to ensure some division of labour between the various agencies concerned with environmental problems. But what is not effectively achieved today (although it has been many times discussed) is a wider coordination: a system for keeping the programmes of the entire system under review, with the aim of seeking to adjust the balance between the parts or to reconsider priorities. At present the balance is the chance result of the decisions reached *within* each agency about its own spending programme. This effectively precludes coordination in the full sense, such as any national government invariably secures in relation to the spending of individual ministries: no such government would think of allowing each ministry to make its own decision about its own level of expenditure without any control from above. In theory ECOSOC, which has been named as the main coordinating body for the system, should perform this role. But in practice ECOSOC has neither the ability nor the opportunity to do so. Above all, it has not the stature to do it, being attended by relatively low-level delegations whose normal concern is almost exclusively with the United Nations itself.

What is really needed, therefore, if the functional activities of the

UN system are to be made more effective, is a new coordinating body that would be the intergovernmental equivalent of the ACC. It would need to be balanced in composition not only between regions in the normal way, but between the United Nations and the agencies, so that the latter could feel they were represented in it and had a chance to influence its decisions. And its members would need to be sufficiently high-powered (possibly ministers within their own governments) for the decisions to carry the weight required. There would have to be an effective follow-up procedure to ensure that, once reached, decisions were effectively implemented. This is a major change which would no doubt encounter strong resistance. But, unless some such initiative is taken, it is likely that interagency coordination will be as feeble in the future as it has shown itself to be in the past.

What is certain is that, if it is to survive, the UN system must show itself capable of responding to new problems and evolving with the international environment. Its capacity to create new institutions, or reform existing ones, will determine how far it can meet the changing needs of a changing society. Whether and how it does so will be a major issue of the global politics of the future.

CONCLUSIONS

The functional tasks of the UN family are likely to grow further in the years ahead. There may be new fields of activity – the allocation of world liquidity, the preservation of the world's environment, the monitoring of transnational corporations, even perhaps the management of the world economy – in which the UN system will be increasingly involved. There will no doubt be proposals, as from time to time in the past, that new bodies should be set up outside the UN framework for that purpose. The aim of such proposals is usually to get away from "third-world dominated" bodies, beset by "conflict" and "inefficiency", to the comfort and convenience of bodies in which the Western states play a dominant part (occasionally the Soviet Union is also accorded a place) and in which, it is believed, a more businesslike and constructive atmosphere would prevail. Such ideas, though understandable, ignore the essential reality that on almost every issue the views and aspirations of third-world countries are an important factor. Whether we like it or not, they must therefore to some extent be involved in discussing and arriving at decisions. Organizations dominated by the West may have a role to play for limited purposes: the IEA can discuss the policies *Western* nations should pursue in the energy field, but not those required in the world as a whole; the OECD can propose economic policies for *Western* states, but not for the third-world or the Eastern bloc.

Where the problems to be confronted are international – and we have seen that usually today they are international – genuinely global bodies are required, which means in practice UN bodies. An attempt can be made within these to ensure that decision-making power is based on the size, population and importance of each state, rather than simply on a one-nation–one-vote basis. Probably this can best be done by seeking to ensure that (as is already the case in most of the agencies today) the council or board of the agency concerned is weighted in favour of larger countries; and that the council enjoys broad executive powers and is partly independent of its assembly. But taking an organization out of the UN family altogether does not assist in this respect. It only complicates relations with other international bodies with which it will almost certainly have to deal. And it will be bitterly resented by most third-world countries which attach importance to the UN link. Still less is a unilateral boycott of a particular organization – as has occurred in the case of UNESCO – a constructive move. In this case, no new, more "efficient" body is established. All that results is that the existing one is weakened, divisions among members – including Western ones – are exacerbated, and all chance of influence is finally forfeited.

A recurrent problem is how to ensure that the many valuable, and mainly non-controversial, activities of these organizations are not disrupted by political conflicts. As we have seen, political controversy cannot be avoided; and it is not realistic for Western states to threaten sanctions or even withdrawal whenever such issues are raised. What is reasonable, however, is to seek to demonstrate, as often and as emphatically as possible, the dangers of repeated harping on extraneous political issues, and the likelihood that raising them in inappropriate places will rarely contribute anything to the solution of the underlying problem but may well antagonize possible sympathizers.

The issue which will remain in the forefront of discussion in all international organizations is the fundamental question: how much should be spent? As we have seen, this is already a highly contentious issue in most of them, with the poor countries calling for more money for more programmes and the richer states of both East and West opposing such calls. There is no objective or universally acceptable answer to this question, and it cannot fail to remain a cause of conflict, in international as in national government. It would be a huge advance if it were possible to arrive at some kind of consensus about the magnitude of increases in expenditure that are generally tolerable *before* decisions on programmes are undertaken. Then the coat, representing the sum total of programmes to be undertaken, would have to be cut according to the total cloth available. Even if such a system could be everywhere established, however – and, in the case of the United Nations itself and some of the agencies at least, this is not perhaps very likely unless on a very informal basis – contentious decisions would still need to be taken about the total volume of expenditure to be allocated for each programme.

Many Western governments continually oppose increases in these budgets. There is, however, a case for saying that money devoted to this purpose is a good investment in international cooperation and development and so in goodwill. Budgetary contributions could be regarded as an element in overall aid programmes (of which they are only a small part).[4] They are probably little less cost-effective than other parts of aid programmes. Part of the money goes in pursuit of aims which benefit the West as much as the third world (for example, better world meteorological services, safer shipping, safer aviation or better telecommunications). Most of the rest is devoted to types of development which almost everybody recognizes to be badly needed: for example, the improvement of world health standards, family planning, or the reduction of illiteracy. It is more logical to try to ensure that the money allocated is spent in the most cost-effective and productive way than to appear stubbornly opposed to any increase in spending at all.

In any political system the type of institutions that are established will reflect the underlying interests and concerns of the main political actors. At present the main conflicts on this question within the global system are between richer and poorer countries. But this will not necessarily always be so. Such conflicts may (as already seen in the controversy over a UN energy agency) reflect the conflicting interests of particular states. And increasingly they may reflect the divergent interests of groups and individuals too. In other words,

4. Because so much is development-related, a fair portion of the sums contributed can reasonably be included in assessments of programme towards the United Nations' aid target of 0·7 per cent of national income to be allocated to official aid.

conflict about the type and scale of the institutions required will, within the global system as within national systems, be one aspect of a wider political struggle, reflecting the underlying political interests of states and individuals alike.

8 The Political Institutions of World Society

The functional bodies which we have been considering, however, have never been regarded as the institutions of greatest importance, either within states or among them. They have generally been seen as peripheral elements within a wider political system: component parts of a structure dominated by more central institutions, of wider authority than any of these could have, essentially political in character and purpose.

It is political institutions of that kind which, it has been generally believed, would, at the international level, have the main responsibility for transforming relationships among states: for resolving conflicts and establishing a more peaceful and stable world society. The belief that some central international institution was required to transform relationships among states goes back many years. In the Middle Ages, the Frenchman, Father Dubois, conceived of a "Council" of Christian sovereigns who would renounce war and agree to settle their disputes by arbitration, recognizing the Pope as final arbiter. In the seventeenth and eighteenth centuries a whole series of blue-prints were put forward for an authority which might resolve the conflicts of states on a peaceful basis. These included Sully's "Grand Design" for maintaining the peace of the continent (and curbing Hapsburg power); William Penn's plan for a "European Diet" bringing together deputies representing the rulers of Europe to settle differences between states not resolved by diplomacy on a system of weighted voting; the Abbé Pierre's plan for a European council which would preserve the territorial *status quo* and even help to suppress revolution within states; Bentham's plan for a Common Court of Judicature to settle disputes between states and a Congress to plan the action to be taken where a state refused to implement a judgement of the court; and Kant's plan for a "perpetual peace" under which all states, under a common republican system of government, would renounce all claims to acquire territory, whether by conquest, inheritance or any other means, and undertake not to borrow money on international markets (which was at that time done almost exclusively for the purpose of making war). None of these plans was implemented, or even taken very seriously. Generally speaking such ideas were less appealing to the rulers who were asked to relinquish their sovereignty than they were to the detached observers who propounded them. The furthest which governments were willing to go was to join, during the nineteenth century, in establishing the more restricted authority of the Concert of Europe, under which the five principal states of the region met regularly to resolve the principal disputes of the area, often deciding the affairs of lesser states as well as their own. The sacrifice of national independence that system called for was only marginal: at least for the major states. None of these was asked to relinquish its treasured sovereignty: only to be willing to meet and discuss and, if possible, in their own mutual interests to reach accommodation with other major states.

It was only with the establishment of the League of Nations in 1919 that a more comprehensive institution was established. Even then the principle of national sovereignty was jealously preserved. It was still an association of states, come together for their mutual benefit, to consider and if possible resolve the principal conflicts of the day. Just as, in the Concert of Europe, it had been accepted that no agreement could be reached among its members unless each gave its individual consent, so now it was laid down that each and every one of the fifty or so members of the organization (except, in theory, a state which was party to a dispute under discussion) could exercise a veto. Nor could any state be constrained or compelled to join in collective action to maintain the peace. Each would decide individually whether it would (as it had undertaken to in the Covenant of the organization) act to "protect as against external aggression the independence and territorial integrity" of other members. In the event each member-state interpreted this undertaking in its own, very restricted way. The effect was that no state ever took up arms for that purpose. The requirements of sovereignty, under which each state determined its own interests in its own way, meant in practice that each decided to do nothing (p. 24 above).

There was another sense in which the new institution was effectively one of, and for, national states. It met to consider the disputes of governments: the local and bi-lateral conflicts of individual national states. On such bi-lateral disputes, it was hoped, most of the other states of the world, not directly involved, would be able to take the position of disinterested bystanders, and so could play the part of impartial judge and jury. The procedures of the organization were thus those of a law court, before which the two parties to a dispute would be called to present their case: at the end of which the assembled Council, or occasionally the Assembly, would pronounce their judgement between the parties. Each party pledged itself to take no armed action while the hearing continued and would take no further action, if still dissatisfied, for a specified period thereafter. The League was able to resolve a number of bi-lateral disputes in this way: between Albania and Yugoslavia, between Lithuania and Poland, between Turkey and Iraq, between Greece and Bulgaria, and between Greece and Italy. But it is not certain that it resolved any conflicts which would otherwise have led to war. The most serious disputes of the day – between Japan and China over Manchuria, between Italy and Ethopia, Italy and Albania, the Soviet Union and Finland, above all between Germany and her neighbours over the Rhineland, Sudetenland, Bohemia and Poland, were not resolved in that way.

The authority of the League was not sufficient to influence a state which was set on national aggrandizement. It would not conciliate a state which refused to be conciliated. Where nationalist ambitions were powerful enough, individual states would cheerfully ignore altogether the procedures laid down. And none of the bystanders were sufficiently concerned, or sufficiently public-spirited, to take up arms, in the way they had pledged to do, to protect the territorial integrity of those states which were attacked.

The new organization established in 1945, at the end of the ensuing conflict, was in theory intended to avoid some of the weaknesses displayed by the League. Greater constraints were placed on national sovereignty. Every member-state was to agree, in becoming a member, to accept the "decisions" of the Security Council, including those demanding the use of force to defend a member-state under attack. Only the five greatest powers, the permanent members, would be spared this sacrifice of sovereignty, since they would be accorded a veto, enabling them to prevent the passage of any resolution (unless they were specifically named as a "party to a dispute", a course the Council chose not to adopt) of which they disapproved. If put into effect, this would have involved a revolutionary relinquishment of national independence by most of the members of the organization. In practice, as we saw (p. 25), they were never asked to make that sacrifice. The Council never made a "decision" under Article 25 of its Charter, calling on the membership to take up arms to defend another under attack. In this way the tradition of national sovereignty, and the restriction this implied on the authority of the organization, was quickly re-established.

Like its predecessor the organization saw its task as the resolution of bi-lateral conflicts among individual states. The provisions of its Charter, relating to the maintenance of peace, consistently spoke of the resolution, by peaceful conciliation or by armed enforcement, of "disputes". These, the uncommitted majority, and above all the combined might of the permanent members, were to bring to a settlement. The Security Council was to institute a whole series of measures – for conciliation, mediation, arbitration, negotiation, if necessary the recommendation of a settlement by the Council itself – to bring the two states concerned to accept a peaceful resolution. The implication was still, as in the days of the League, that there would be only two states in conflict, or at most a very small group: the great majority would then together intercede impartially between them in order to bring them to reason.

That conception did not allow for the globalization of politics which had occurred. The conflicts of the post-war age were no longer the simple, isolated, local, bilateral issues between individual sovereign states, of the kind which had occurred at the time of the League. It was no longer a question of two isolated antagonists, surrounded by a great majority of disinterested bystanders. There were now few bystanders, because almost all were part of the battle. The shrinkage of distance had the effect that the entire world was now a single political battlefield. A large proportion of the world's states were arrayed in large-scale alliances, ranged in uncompromising hostility to each other. Almost every incident, wherever it occurred, was seen as of direct and immediate consequence to one side or the other, and usually to both. The globalization of politics thus destroyed one of the essential premises of the system; that the new central political institution could act as an impartial judge of the misdemeanors of one or two squabbling, misbehaved delinquents. The central institution was not above the conflict, able to maintain order by injunctions from afar. It was the central arena within which the conflict took place.

Nor were all the conflicts in the world-wide political system between states at all. Some of the most important actors of the political world were now non-state actors, intensifying, complicating, or even cross-cutting the conflicts of states, yet not themselves represented in the new institution. Huge economic organizations, transnational banks and industrial corporations, were now "beyond sovereignty", operating in a large number of states, acquiring great economic power within some of them, yet often not clearly based in any single state and so able to escape the jurisdiction (and the taxation) of any single government. Large-scale political movements – Islamic fundamentalists, or terrorist groups, or secessionist movements within states – became significant participants in world politics, and occasionally involved in major conflicts among states. Yet they too were not represented within world organizations. Single-issue groupings, such as the Green movement, disarmament and human rights groups, operating across national boundaries, were of considerable political significance, but again had no direct representation. Only national governments were represented. And only in so far as those governments were themselves representative of their populations, could the voice of individuals and particular groups among them, make themselves heard within the organization.

There was another important reason why the world which emerged after 1945 differed from that anticipated in the UN's Charter. That document was created by states and for states. Conflicts *within* states were rigorously excluded from its discussions. The tradition of sovereignty still demanded that these should be seen as the exclusive responsibility of the government of the state concerned: conflicts into which the organization should not presume to interfere. It was on these grounds laid down that the organization was not to "intervene in matters essentially within the domestic jurisdiction of a member-state". But in the post-war world the vast majority of wars were precisely of this kind. In practice few of them were entirely domestic. In many cases there was substantial intervention from one source or another so that eventually (as in Vietnam and Afghanistan, Lebanon and Angola, for example) the forces involved, or at least the most powerful of them, were those of the outside states rather than those of the domestic factions. Yet they remained, formally, civil wars and so, in theory, beyond the authority of the organization. So it was that some of the most bitter and costly conflicts of the day – in Vietnam, Nigeria, Cambodia, El Salvador, Angola, Mozambique and Ethiopia among many others – remained almost entirely unconsidered by the organization; or, if they were raised at all, were declared by the government concerned and its supporters to be beyond its competence.

There was, finally, yet another reason why the new organization was not able to confront effectively many of the most important issues of the day. It was seen by most states as concerned only with questions of peace and war. Its Security Council was explicitly enjoined to be responsible for matters of international peace and security. But many of the most significant disputes among states were now economic conflicts: concerning debt, investment, trade, aid, and other such questions. Because they did normally lead to war these were not considered by the Security Council. They were sometimes discussed, though briefly and inconclusively, and unknown to the general public, in the General Assembly's Second Committee (which did concern itself with economic questions). But for the most part they were ignored within the United Nations since, it was believed, they were more properly the responsibility of the specialized agencies and similar bodies, in some cases specifically concerned with such questions. But those bodies, as we have seen, were not under the effective authority of the UN itself, and only loosely related with each other. Most of the economic conflicts had political overtones (just as political conflicts sometimes had economic roots). And it is arguable that in a world in which many of the principal disputes among states were economic in character, they should have come more regularly and systematically under discussion in the central political institution of the system.

The international political system had thus become something very different from what had been anticipated in 1945. It was no longer exclusively a system of national states, each occasionally involved in a conflict with some other state. It was rather a global political system producing innumerable local conflicts, often involving groups and individuals rather than states; within and across countries rather than between them; transnational rather than international. It was no longer a world of isolated homogeneous national units, interacting with similar national units. It was rather a complex web of transactions transcending national boundaries, in which some of the most important actors were not states at all but a variety of non-state entities – individuals, groups, political organizations, revolutionary movements, multinational banks and companies, world-wide federations of workers, scientists or campaigners, international organizations of every kind. An authority designed only to solve the conflicts of states with each other was not necessarily well adapted to meet the problems which arose in such a world.

THE GLOBALIZATION OF CONFLICT

The globalization of politics reflected the globalization of conflict.

Both the sources of conflict and its character had become altogether different from what they had been in earlier days.

The political struggle today takes place within an arena which comprehends the world as a whole. The welfare of one state's citizens is affected almost as much by the type of government which comes to power in a neighbouring country as by the type of government which rules them in their own. Their fortunes may be affected by the actions of a crusading, anti-communist president in the US, or of a Soviet leader seeking to spread Marxist doctrine and Soviet power to other parts of the world, more than they are by any policies their own government pursues. And the types of relationship established between two such leaders – hostile or harmonious – will affect the peoples of other countries almost as much as it will affect those of their own. Conversely, for those superpowers themselves the ideological complexion of governments in other states becomes of acute strategic and political importance. The emergence of a new government of opposing ideology in another country may be seen as a challenge or even a threat; the emergence of one that is ideologically sympathetic may be seen as a victory and a reassurance. Political and ideological concerns, which were previously concentrated within a single state, now become world-wide.

But political struggle in the modern world is not only global but transnational. It involves not only states but groups and individuals as well. States are not homogeneous entities that can be crudely classified as "communist" or "anti-communist", liberal or conservative, nationalist or internationalist. Each is an assemblage of large numbers of diverse human beings of widely varying viewpoints. The policies and positions which are supported by the majority of one state will be supported by a minority in another. With modern communications systems political ideas are transmitted quickly from one country to another. Transnational political movements thus develop, seeking political change in a number of countries simultaneously. Groups and individuals, like governments, acquire wider political horizons. They are no longer concerned only about seeking political change in their own country. They seek political change in others as well.

Political conflict becomes transnational for other reasons. Political *interests* are globalized. Because transnational corporations, industrial and commercial, are no longer closely rooted in a single national economy but operate simultaneously in a large number of countries, their interests become non-national. Because transnational banks and other financial institutions transfer vast funds across frontiers they too cease to be identified with any particular country. Workers and consumers too, as a result, acquire interests that are transnational. Unions are obliged to organize themselves on an international basis, to match the dispersed operations of the big corporations: in the ICFTU (International Confederation of Free Trade Unions), the International Metalworkers Union, and similar bodies. Consumers must work to make their views effective, not only in the framework of the national state but far beyond: as consumer organizations do already today within the institutions of the EEC.

Because interests increasingly cross state boundaries, so does political conflict. The institutions set up to resolve political disputes must therefore be equipped to deal with transnational conflict. In the economic field they must be able to deal not only with direct interstate disputes on tariffs and trade, monetary questions and aid (as traditionally dealt with by the General Agreement on Tariffs and Trade (GATT), the IMF and the World Bank respectively) – but with conflicts concerning the transfer of technology or the investment and labour policies of international companies (as are now already sometimes dealt with by the UN Commission on Transnational Corporations, the UN Conference on Trade and Development (UNCTAD) and the ILO). In the political field too effective institutions must be equipped to deal with political struggles which take place transnationally as well as internationally: across frontiers as well as against them; by world-wide political movements within a number of states as well as by one state against another.

This means that the responsibilities of international institutions are broadened. To operate effectively they have to be concerned with many matters once regarded as of local interest only: must be as concerned about conflicts which appear to be "domestic" as about those which are fully international. In modern conditions the distinction between international and domestic disputes becomes almost impossible to draw. Many conflicts which are designated as "civil wars" are, both in their causes and their effects, partly international.

Often their *cause* is partly external. They may have been deliberately instigated by outside governments or agencies, seeking to promote political change within the state concerned. At the very least they are intensified by the actions of other states: through large-scale military and other assistance given to one side or the other, or both.

But they are also international in their *effect*. The instability created by war in one country affects the stability of its neighbours (as for example in South-East Asia, Central America or Southern Africa in recent times). And the final victory of one side or another may have vital consequences for neighbouring countries; or at least may be feared likely to do so.

Civil conflicts, therefore, can no longer be seen as local affairs which can be ignored by international organizations; or, if considered by them at all, seen as isolated events, divorced from world-wide political currents which can be separately resolved. They are elements within an interrelated world political process. So the war in South Vietnam was dominated by external actors (North Vietnam and her allies, the US and hers) and in turn spilled over into Cambodia and Laos. War in Nicaragua is conducted mainly from outside that state but in turn influences other states of the region. War in Mozambique and Angola is instigated by an outside power but affects Zimbabwe, Malawi and Tanzania. There is no clear boundary to such conflicts, defined by national borders. Though all may originally have had local causes, they become part of a much wider political struggle.

As a result the distinction between civil and international war becomes meaningless. Traditionally international law drew a sharp line between civil wars, in which no external power was supposed to interfere, and international conflicts which were the concern of all states. International organizations, set up by national states insisting on the principle of "sovereignty", made much of that distinction. So the League of Nations turned its eyes resolutley away from the civil wars taking place in a number of countries of the world in its day on the grounds that they were beyond international jurisdiction: even in Spain where foreign intervention was massive and acknowledged. The United Nations, having insisted, as we saw, on its foundation, that nothing within the Charter gave the organization the right to intervene in matters within domestic jurisdiction, also often refrained from considering civil war situations.

In the modern world that distinction has become unsustainable. In practice the United Nations, whatever its Charter declares, has found itself obliged to involve itself in many conflicts which were primarily domestic in character: for example in Greece in 1946–9, in Lebanon and Jordan in 1958, in the Congo in 1960–4, in the Yemen in 1962–7, in Cyprus from 1964 onwards and the Lebanon from 1978 on, to name only a few (in addition to numerous colonial conflicts which in legal terms were also domestic in character). Sometimes it found it necessary to claim evidence of external involvement in such conflicts. But in modern conditions, where some degree of foreign involvement – even if it is only the supply of arms – occurs almost everywhere, evidence of that sort is not difficult to find. It is thus now widely recognized that most civil conflicts are partly international; and must sometimes come under international attention if world order is to be maintained. Indeed, since the vast majority of the wars of the modern world are civil conflicts, at least in origin (the Iraq–Iran war is perhaps the only notable exception in recent years), the organization would have little to do if it were not willing occasionally to devote its attention to such conflicts.

External intervention in such wars has had obvious attractions. Their outcome, determining what type of government holds power in a particular state, often appears of vital importance to the national security or political interest of outside powers. These therefore may seek to protect those interests, at little direct cost to themselves, by discrete intervention in the struggles of other states, rather than by direct attacks against each other. So purely local conflicts are often hugely magnified by the scale of external intervention, often on both sides: as in Vietnam, Afghanistan, Cyprus, Lebanon, Mozambique, Angola, Nicaragua and Cambodia, to name only a few of the more obvious examples of recent years. Where intervention is by a superpower, on one or both sides, the dangers are particularly obvious. But even where it is undertaken by lesser powers – as by Egypt in Yemen, by South Africa in Angola and Mozambique, by Syria and Israel in Lebanon – the effect is still deeply destabilizing and a threat to world peace. As improved military mobility makes rapid action in any part of the world even easier, the attractions of such activity increase. If major powers can secure their most important objectives – the overthrow of a hostile government, the seizure of power by a congenial faction in a politically sensitive state – by such relatively risk-free means, it is scarcely surprising that it is a course of action which is frequently adopted.

Contemporary international institutions require, therefore, to be equipped above all to deal with conflicts of that type. Existing bodies have not so far proved well equipped for that task. At a time when conflict has increasingly become transnational rather than international, intrafrontier rather than transfrontier, the United Nations continues to operate on the basis of national sovereignty. It can scarcely fail to do this because it is established on the basis of the representation of national states. Both the United Nations itself and its associated agencies are associations of states, rather than of peoples. This affects their response to the conflicts with which they are confronted in a number of ways.

The initial response to the conflicts of the age is in terms of national political interests. There is little attempt to look at the underlying roots of each conflict: at the social, political and economic conditions which have caused it. Each issue is seen not as one affecting peoples, or even societies, but as one among governments. Thus every other government, and every alliance of governments, will support those governments with which they are politically in sympathy, and denounce the activities of those to which they are opposed. Instead of an attempt to make an objective appraisal of each situation as it arises and to devise the response which is appropriate, the first instinct is to seek a public condemnation of the governments that are opponents, or a public endorsement for governments that are friends. Intensive lobbying is undertaken to win the votes of the uncommitted, and the outcome is not so much to procure a final settlement of complex problems, often transcending the boundaries of many countries, as to win the contest: to score, as in a computer game, the maximum total in the tally of votes finally achieved. The basis of the approach is confrontation rather than cooperation, an attempt to win a resounding victory over opponents rather than a lasting settlement of fundamental problems: to promote the national interest or the alliance interest rather than the public interest. This affects the financial and functional bodies of the organization, as much as the political institutions. Here too blocks are formed to represent the interests of rich states and, poor, European countries and Afro-Asian, producers and consumers. And here, too, there is nobody present to represent the vast mass of ordinary human beings, whose interests are not necessarily reflected in the stereotyped attitudes of the assembled national governments.

The second effect of the state-oriented character of existing international authority is the overriding concern with sovereignty. However divided they may be on other questions, member-states are united in their belief that international bodies should not be allowed, in essentials, to challenge the authority of the national state. They continue to demand that, at the end of the day, each individual government can determine for itself whether or not it will accept a proposal which may infringe its own national independence. Thus though, on occasion, members may be willing to demand actions threatening the sovereignty of *other* states – demanding, for example, an end to colonialism, or the abolition of apartheid in South Africa – they will uniformly resist moves that threaten the sovereignty of their own. This not only means that they normally deny the right of the organization to consider civil conflicts taking place within their own borders. They challenge its authority in other fields equally – whether related to their right to impose trade restrictions, the protection of human rights, economic and social politics, the protection of the environment – if they regard its demands as contrary to their interests.

A third consequence of the state-related approach is the insistence on the principle of one-nation one-vote. Because the United Nations (and its agencies) are organizations of nation-states, membership is based on the principle of "sovereign equality", and decisions are based on the fiction that all states are equal. Though a few of the more powerful states can exercise a veto within the Security Council, their votes remain equal to those of others whenever a resolution is voted on. This has the effect that the representative of the United States has an exactly equal voice with those of Mali and the Maldives, the representative of the Soviet Union has an equal voice with that of the Solomons and St Kitts; that China, with a population of a billion, has a voice equal with that of a state with a population only 20,000th as large; that the 50 countries of Africa have a voice many times greater than can China, with a population double that of their combined peoples. Such a system inevitably breeds cynicism. It becomes easy to challenge the significance of resolutions passed in that way; the public then doubt the authority of the organization where decisions are made. Only a body which is more genuinely representative of the balance of international opinion, it is widely believed, could exercise greater influence on the actions of states.

In a number of ways, therefore, contemporary international institutions are poorly equipped to deal with a world of global politics; a world where conflict is transnational rather than international, and a world where many of the most important participants are no longer states but the individual citizens and groups of which states are composed. Only reformed institutions are likely to be able to regain the confidence which existing bodies no longer enjoy.

THE FRAGMENTARY CHARACTER OF CONTEMPORARY INSTITUTIONS

If the types of conflict that mainly occur in the modern world are to be dealt with effectively, a different type of international authority may be required.

There are a number of important differences between the way authority is exercised at the international level and the authority wielded by national states.

First, governments within states exercise authority directly over each individual who resides within their territory. Their right to exercise authority is rarely questioned; and their power to enforce that right if necessary is in any case so overwhelming that it is to a large extent unchallengeable. In international society political institutions enjoy no such power. Any authority they have is exercised only indirectly: not on individual citizens but on the governments who take responsibility for their fortunes. Even over governments their power is extremely limited. Their right to exercise authority is questionable and frequently challenged. The doctrine of national "sovereignty" means that international bodies can normally secure their will only in so far as governments voluntarily accept it. Since international bodies lack the physical power to enforce their authority where necessary, the national state is, in the final resort, in a position to defy their demands. On the most important questions of all it will do so.

Secondly, international authority, even in those fields where most states concede it some legitimacy, is divided. Within states parliaments are normally supreme. Whatever degree of independence is accorded to the judicature, judges must in practice apply the laws that are enacted by the legislature. The theoretical "division of powers" does not alter the fact that in the final resort the former can dictate to the latter (even if ultimately it may require to secure a change in the constitution to do so). In international society there is no source of ultimate authority, comparable to that within states. The General Assembly of the United Nations cannot legislate. The effect in international law of its resolutions, even of its "Declarations", passed by overwhelming majorities, is questioned by many. They are not binding on the International Court of Justice. Conversely, though the International Court may give "advisory opinions" to UN bodies if requested to do so, these too are not binding on the latter. The relationship between "legislature" and "judiciary" is thus, within the international system, an indeterminate one. In this case there is no means by which the legislature – that is, the General Assembly – can exercise ultimate authority.

Nor are executive bodies any more directly subject to the legislature. The relationship between the Security Council, often seen as the UN's chief "executive" body, at least in the security field, and the Assembly, the main deliberative body, is ambiguous. Under the Charter the Security Council has the "primary responsibility" for the maintenance of international peace and security. The Assembly is not supposed to discuss any question which is at the same time under active consideration by the Council. Yet at the same time the Assembly is empowered to discuss anything "within the scope of the Charter"; and in practice, despite the Charter's injunction, frequently discusses issues and disputes which are also being considered by the Security Council. The Assembly can pass recommendations to the Council. But it cannot determine its actions nor, conversely, can the Council instruct the Assembly on the actions it is to take.

The relationship between the United Nations as a whole and the specialized agencies, which also exercise executive powers in particular fields, is a still looser one. The latter are said to be part of the UN "family" or "system"; yet at the same time they are "autonomous". In all but name they are totally independent bodies, with their own assemblies and councils, which are not accountable to the United Nations or any other body. Though there is supposed to be a system of "coordination", designed to prevent overlap and bring about some general coherence in the policies of all organizations within the system, this is so loose as to be almost imperceptible. They cannot be given instructions by any organ of the United Nations proper; and when the Assembly has attempted to do so – for example seeking to instruct them concerning their policies towards South Africa – the agencies have on occasions point-blank refused to comply with their injunctions.

Neither judiciary, nor executive, therefore, is in any immediate sense under the authority of the central representative institution of the system. Still less do local – that is regional – bodies come under the direct authority of the Assembly, or even of the United Nations at all. Such bodies as the Organization of American States (OAS), the Organization of African Unity (OAU), the Association of South-East Asian Nations (ASEAN) and the European Community are not even a part of the UN system at all. They are separate bodies which operate, at their own level, entirely independently of the wider international institutions.

But, thirdly, not only is the general framework of world political institutions fragmented and diffused. There is no system by which coherent policy can easily be articulated. Within states this function is undertaken by the central organs of government. A cabinet or a council of ministers implements a known set of policies, often clearly set out in a government programme. And they are in a position, through their control of the state's enforcement agencies, to ensure that those policies are effectively fulfilled, not only by the organs of the state but by all citizens under their authority. In international institutions there is no means by which a coherent set of policies can either be formulated or put into effect. There is no central body capable of drawing up such a programme and ensuring that it is carried out. This is true not only of the wider UN "system", where each functional agency is autonomous and formulates its own programme, almost entirely independently of each other. Even within the UN proper each "commission", or "centre", and even each committee of the General Assembly, formulates its own programme independently, without any serious attempt at central coordination or control. And the despairing efforts of ECOSOC (the Economic and Social Council), and the Committee on Programmes and Coordination (CPC) to establish some kind of coherence on the programmes of different units and committees have, as we saw in the previous chapter, so far been almost entirely without effect.

Within national states integration of this kind is imposed largely through the political programme of the ruling party. This lays down before elections the general framework of policy which it will pursue during its term of office; and it is elaborated in more detailed form by the cabinet or council of ministers in announcing its programme of legislation for the following year or years. Within international institutions there is no political programme which can provide coherence or a common purpose. There is no majority party, with a recognizable programme of its own, informing every decision reached on a wide range of issues, as within national governments. Even when there is a majority group of governments, such as the so-called Group of 77, cooperating for certain purposes, it does not normally seek to establish an agreed programme of that kind because, even within that group (which now consists of nearly 130 governments or three-quarters of the world), there is not sufficient unanimity of view or purpose to formulate a clear-cut body of policies. Some hold right-wing and some left-wing views. Some fear to antagonize the US, some the Soviet Union. Some demand a rapid extension of international authority, some fear it. In effect, both within and outside its group, each government pursues its own policies independently. And in those circumstances, not surprisingly, no consistent policy or programme of action is carried out, either within any particular international body, or still less, in all of them. Nor, even if there were, could this majority necessarily secure the compliance of the remaining governments, which remain ultimately independent. For example, although, over recent years, a majority of member-states in the United Nations have advocated the establishment of a "new international economic order", perhaps the first clearly articulated programme proposed by a major group of states, they have not been in a position to make that programme effective because the minority of powerful states which held the purse strings refused to cooperate.

The incoherence of the existing international institutional structure is made still greater as a result of straightforward political disputes. These may divide large numbers of governments according to their political viewpoint: communist against anti-communist, liberal against authoritarian, religious against secular, progressive against conservative, rich country against poor. Or they may be regional in character: dividing East European and West European, African and Latin American, East Asian and South Asian. Or they may be local and individual conflicts: for example the division between the Arab states and Israel and their supporters, between South Africa and other African countries; or immediate bilateral antagonisms – as between India and Pakistan, Iraq and Iran, Vietnam and Thailand, and so on. Political conflicts of all these types, which are endemic, exercise a major influence on the support given by individual states to alternative policy proposals. And these too inhibit the establishment of clearly defined political groupings, each committed to their own programmes.

So the process of international decision-making is further complicated. The majority which may exist for one particular proposal does not exist for another. The most that can be established are *ad hoc* coalitions on particular issues and propositions. The system is thus more akin to that of eighteenth-century politics in Britain, with several hundred independent members of parliament grouping themselves into *ad hoc* factions and caucuses, rather than of any contemporary parliament, in which the majority are members of distinctive political parties, closely committed to the detailed programmes of action espoused by those parties. Within international institutions, as in the British parliament in the eighteenth century, factionalism is the central principle of political organization. And support for a particular proposal by each faction may be bargained for; even bought and sold – if not for money then at least against support for some other proposition, required as a quid pro quo by those offering their votes.

Then there are the additional problems which result from the high degree of bureaucratic power in international organizations. In many cases the principal intergovernmental bodies meet at relatively long intervals: the assemblies of most of the specialized agencies for a month or so every two or three years, that of the United Nations only for three months a year, and so on. Although often the executive "councils" meet more frequently – at least once a quarter, and sometimes every month or so – their meetings are still not frequent enough for any close sense of common purpose or collective responsibility to be established. They remain occasional gatherings of representatives of assorted governments of widely varying views. In the meantime, inevitably, power falls into the hands of those on the spot. Day-to-day actions and decisions still have to be taken – even if in theory, within the framework of the decisions of the intergovernmental bodies. This is done by the executive heads and other senior officials of each agency. Because the guidelines are expressed in long and complex resolutions, there exists a considerable latitude for interpretation. The executive heads therefore acquire very considerable power. Some of them become in effect small-scale dictators, able to guide and manipulate the less knowledgeable representatives of member governments (just as their opposite numbers within states can frequently manipulate ministers in their own system). In this way they are in a position to impose their own viewpoint on the programmes and policies of the organization. This power is enhanced by their ability to appoint and dismiss officials, and reallocate duties within the organization. So, often, organizational politics become as important as intergovernmental politics. This further complicates the political process within such institutions.

There is another characteristic of international government which differentiates it from the process which occurs within states. In national governments the process of *deliberation*, undertaken by parliaments, is clearly differentiated from that of *decision-making*, undertaken by cabinets and cabinet committees. In general the decision-making institutions and procedures have become largely independent of the former, and have even acquired a greater authority. As a result, the power of parliaments has steadily declined before that of the executive (the independence of the former eroded by the fact that the majority of members of parliament are often now closely linked, by political allegiance and hope of advancement, to the government of the day). In international bodies, on the other hand, it is the deliberative institutions – the assemblies – and their procedures – public discussion – which still dominate the scene. Vast amounts of time and energy are expended on sterile public debate, which often leads to no significant outcome; while the decisions taken – if any – result often from bureaucratic action, largely unseen by the public as a whole.

A major difference concerns the *visibility* of the two processes. In the national system of government the disagreements which lie behind decisions on policy – within the cabinet room, between two ministries, or among the officials of the same ministry – are unknown to the public. In international government the reverse is the case. It is the argument that is publicized – that in the General Assembly or the Security Council, where it often occurs in the full glare of television lights: over the action to be taken to meet a new threat to the peace, over the election of a new director-general, over the establishment of a new peace-keeping force. In national governments decisions usually come first, and public discussion about whether they were right or wrong come later. In international government the argument comes first; and often prevents any decision being taken at all. Decision-making and deliberation, instead of being two entirely separate procedures, are here merged into a single process: they take place – for example in the Security Council – at the same meeting, among the same group of people, often in the course of a single session. Thus an occasion for decisions, which should be one of deliberate and considered judgement, is instead one of angry confrontation and sterile recrimination. And because the decision is reached in the full glare of publicity, it is seen as an opportunity to put forward national positions rather than international solutions; to strike a posture rather than to seek a compromise. If a decision can be reached at all, therefore, it is likely to be a fudge, composed of a compromise between conflicting national positions, rather than the clear-cut, well-thought-out initiative which may be required.

This decisively influences public perceptions of international institutions. Within national systems, not only are disagreements within the decision-making authority withheld from the public gaze. Once the decisions are reached they are collectively supported, and carefully explained and justified to the public, sometimes by high-powered public relations techniques. In international society, not only are the bodies that reach decisions visibly and publicly divided, so that they can be challenged after the event even by those who took part in the discussion (which cannot be done by the cabinet minister defeated in cabinet). Little or no attempt is made to publicize and explain any decision which may ultimately be reached. The fact that the decision-making body is politically divided means that its decisions do not secure the *legitimacy* which is gained by the decision of a national parliament or a national cabinet, the authority of which is rarely questioned. The decisions which are reached internationally are often scarcely known to the public and are certainly unlikely to be accorded any special reverence.

This lack of legitimacy results fundamentally from the fact that international bodies cannot base their claims to authority, as many national governments do, on the claim to be representative of the people as a whole. National governments which have been democratically elected can legitimately assert that claim. But it is often made also, however spuriously, by governments which have not been elected: these too usually assert that, by whatever means they came to power, they represent the underlying aspirations and interests of their people. International organizations cannot make this claim to legitimacy. Within them states are represented by the governments which hold power there, by whatever means they acquired that power. A considerable proportion of the governments represented have not been elected in free and fair elections, and often not elected at all. Their right to speak for their people may be challenged by a majority of their own population. Other member-states therefore, and their citizens, may reasonably challenge the authority of an organization in which most of the governments represented can make no credible claim to be representative of their peoples. And they can do so, equally cogently, on the grounds that the principle of one-state–one-vote makes the organization unrepresentative in another sense; in that a totally disproportionate power is given to many small and insignificant states, and so indirectly to their populations. Both arguments provide legitimate reasons for challenging, or even rejecting, the authority claimed by such bodies: reasons which are frequently employed.

Underlying all these problems is the most obvious of all (even if it is not as fundamental as is sometimes believed): the lack of enforcement powers available to international bodies. National governments are able to take decisions with confidence, since they know that they have at their disposal unchallengeable power to make their decisions effective (at least within their own frontiers). International bodies have no power of that kind. At the global level political bodies and functional agencies alike must either seek to secure consensus, which means that they can only take the minimal steps which are acceptable to all; or, if a decision is nonetheless forced through, accept that the minority which opposes it may refuse to cooperate altogether. In either case their authority is irretrievably weakened. A refusal to comply with a resolution can be presented by the state concerned as an act of noble defiance or of commendable national independence. The majority which has supported it may be denounced as misguided, tyrannical or unrepresentative. As a result, the widespread public *respect*, which is the fundamental basis on which all authority ultimately rests and the source of its legitimacy, is here not available.

The structure of international authority therefore is incoherent and confused. The capacity for effective decision-making is weak. Conflict within and between some of the principal decision-making bodies is endemic. Legitimacy is low or non-existent. Public respect is lacking. In a word authority is marginal.

THE REFORM OF GLOBAL INSTITUTIONS

If the problems which affect the modern citizen – from drugs traffic to terrorism, from famine to recession, from Aids to refugees – and the conflicts that endanger world peace, are now global, not national in scope, there can be no more important political objective than the reform of the institutions by which those problems are confronted.

The first need is to make them more representative of humankind than they are today. There is no likelihood that they will, in the foreseeable future, be made directly representative of peoples rather than states. It would take a transformation of both state institutions and international bodies more fundamental than any that can now be foreseen for a change of that kind to come about. But even if for the present they remain representative of states, they could still be made more representative of the peoples of the world than the international bodies that exist today.

The most obvious way in which such bodies are unrepresentative today is through the convention of one-state–one-vote. The simplest way of reducing the unrepresentative character of the UN's General Assembly, and of the corresponding assemblies of the agencies, would therefore be by some system for the weighting of votes. There is no doubt that such a system, whether based on population, annual income, or financial contributions to the organization concerned, would be strongly resisted by many member-states today, since the great majority manifestly benefit from the present unrepresentative system. They might, however, if made more aware of the degree to which the current system discredits the organizations, to which they attach great value, be willing to accept some lesser alteration to the current system. For certain votes at least – perhaps for the "important questions" for which a two-thirds majority in the Assembly is already required – a weighting of votes might be accepted. A system might be adopted which, without taking full account of differences in population, national income and so on, might marginally reflect them. Weighting of a kind already exists: the Soviet Union in practice wields three votes, since Byelorussia and the Ukraine are separately represented within the UN. That privilege could be extended to other states of similar size: perhaps those with populations of more than 100 million. Those with populations of more than ten million might have two; and the rest one. In time, possibly, a more radical system of weighting might become acceptable.

But this would affect only votes in the General Assembly, the decisions of which anyway are of only marginal significance. It is more important that the Security Council should be made more representative than it is today. Unrepresentativeness here takes two forms at present. On the one hand the privilege of permanent membership is at present held by only five states: the US, the Soviet Union and China, which obviously merit that position, and by Britain, and France, which are no more deserving of it than half-a-dozen other major countries. This leads to a maldistribution of such seats among continents: Africa and Latin America have no permanent seats, Asia, with two-thirds of the population of the world, has only one, while West Europe, with under a tenth has two. A more balanced representation could be secured by adopting the system, used in the League of Nations, of "semi-permanent" seats; so that, for example, Britain and France, Germany and Italy, Brazil and Argentina, India and Japan, Nigeria and Egypt, shared seats, which would rotate between them every two years.

The second source of malrepresentation is the fact that, despite the injunction in the Charter that, in electing non-permanent members of the Security Council, due regard should be "specially paid, in the first instance, to the contribution of Members of the United Nations to the maintenance of international peace and security, and to the other purposes of the Organization", a number of seats are frequently held by very small states, whose effective contribution in the maintenance of international peace and security is virtually nil. Though small states can reasonably expect occasionally to hold such a seat, it is important that the regional groups which elect to these positions ensure that most of them are held by states of substance, representing substantial populations.

However it is constituted, the Council will only be in a position to confront the scale of conflict in the contemporary world if it operates on a far more continuous basis than it does today. At present its conduct is entirely reactive; it meets to consider conflict situations only at the request of a member-state, nearly always after a conflict has already begun. Contrary to the provisions of the Charter, it never attempts to bring about a process of conciliation in the early stages of a dispute, before armed conflict has begun. The series of measures set out in Chapter VI of the Charter providing for the peaceful settlement of disputes is almost never put into operation today. Often the Council gives the appearance of being caught by surprise: it seeks to deal with an act of force only after fighting has already begun, when it is difficult, if not impossible to bring about a reconciliation. It is therefore left in the position of issuing imploring calls for a ceasefire, or inviting a representative of the Secretary-General to fly forlornly from capital to capital, long after it is too late for him to have any effect.

To operate effectively the Council would need to undertake a continuous monitoring of the international situation, so that it was in a position to intervene at a much earlier stage than it does today. Since most wars today begin as civil conflicts, which increasingly become internationalized, even civil wars would need to be confronted in their early stages (rather than, as at present, if at all, only where external intervention has reached massive proportions). To be in a position to perform this monitoring effectively, the organization would need to maintain a constant watch on the security situation in every part of the world. It would need a staff in New York, comparable to that of foreign offices in national capitals, whose task was to keep the situation in particular areas under regular review. The Secretary-General might appoint representatives in particular regions affected by conflict – such as, for example, Central America, Southern Africa or South-East Asia today – or permanently in each region, as his ambassadors or "special representatives". These would report regularly on developments in each area, and could act on his behalf in making representations to governments where necessary.

The Secretary-General would, as a result, be in a far better position than he is today to alert the Council, and to call on it to take action in particular trouble-spots before a situation of all-out war has been reached.

Another need is for some or all Security Council meetings to be undertaken in private. The effect of public debate is that discussions are used more for an airing of political attitudes, for accusations and counter-accusations, than for a sober examination of the opportunities for constructive influence and fruitful mediation. It is everywhere taken for granted that the pinnacle of achievement for the Council is the passage of a resolution. A huge amount of time and energy is directed to deciding the precise wording of such resolutions, the proposal of amendments, or the devising of rival resolutions, rather than to setting in motion procedures which may lead to a settlement. The latter is not an easy undertaking, whatever the procedure used. But it is certainly not facilitated by the procedures at present adopted. If the Council habitually met in private, there would be no temptation to play to the gallery. There would be more opportunity for the organization of direct conciliation between the parties, which can alone produce results. Above all there might emerge, in the minds of the participants and the public alike, a greater sense of common purpose among the members of the Council, of "collegiality"; a joint endeavour to promote the public interest. In that way one of the essential requirements of an effective authority, the respect due to a public body fulfilling recognizable needs on behalf of society as a whole, might be fulfilled.

That conception might also be promoted if a larger role were given to international officials in implementing the policies agreed. The main lines of the action to be taken – mediation between two states in conflict, the establishment of a new peace-keeping force, the launching of a new disarmament initiative – would be determined by the intergovernmental body concerned (such as the Security Council). But a larger role than at present might then be given to the Secretary-General and his staff in implementing those directives. This is what was done in effect in the days of Dag Hammarskjöld, who was allowed considerable leeway in fulfilling the tasks laid down by the intergovernmental bodies. It may be necessary, if international tasks are to be performed with greater flexibility and independence, for a similar course to be pursued today. Conversely, the Secretary-General himself may need to be more self-confident in proposing particular measures when the intergovernmental bodies are failing to take action. At least he should be more willing to call for a meeting of the Security Council to meet a particular threat (as he is entitled to do under Article 99 of the Charter).

Even more necessary, if the authority of international bodies is to be built up over the years, is the progressive development of a body of principles governing conduct among states. A considerable proportion of interstate conflict in the modern world results from ambiguous forms of activity for which no recognized rules exist. A classic case is forcible intervention of various kinds in civil conflicts in other states: a question on which international law has been uncertain and disputed for many years. Such intervention may be said by the intervening state to be necessary to protect a government under threat, to assist those legitimately rebelling against an unrepresentative government, or to "maintain law and order" generally. Since no clear-cut rules have been established on the question by the international community such justifications remain permanently available to states wishing to intervene. By establishing a generally accepted set of principles governing international behaviour in the modern world, international bodies might in time become able to regulate the at present disordered character of national behaviour and provide the rules of interaction which an orderly society requires.

Ultimately more radical changes may be required. An organization that is representative only of governments may cease to be able to command the respect and support of many groups and individuals which reject the authority of those governments; their own as well as others. The United Nations under its present constitution may increasingly be denounced as an illegitimate body, deriving its authority only from the power asserted by governments, rather than from the consent of the governed or the free choice of peoples. If a world authority that is directly elected is not at present feasible, at least other ways might be found by which the views of the general public can make themselves felt. New channels might be created by which interested groups could exercise a voice in the decisions reached by international organizations.

So far that principle has only been marginally recognized: in the arrangements made for consulting non-governmental organizations and for the "forums" established at the time of major intergovernmental conferences (p. 69). On those occasions non-governmental organizations have been able to organize discussions of their own on many of the same questions being discussed at the official meetings and to express their own points of view. Those views have sometimes, it can reasonably be claimed, been more representative of public opinion generally than those expressed by governments.

It would not be impossible to apply similar methods to the discussion of political issues. Meetings could be organized in New York at the time of the annual General Assembly, in the autumn of each year, at which a range of unofficial groups might be enabled to discuss similar topics to those being discussed at the Assembly. A simple method of providing some opportunity for the expression of non-governmental views would be to arrange that the annual conferences of the Inter-Parliamentary Union, in which both government and opposition parties in all the parliaments of the world are represented, were to meet at the same time as the Assembly and would then discuss similar issues. Specialized interest-groups might be brought together to hold similar debates, or at least to influence the discussions being undertaken by governments on particular topics.

It would also be possible to provide permanent fora for particular interest-groups. The European community has established such a specialized body: the Economic and Social Committee, in which trade unions, employers' organizations, and consumer associations, among others, are represented, to discuss major social and economic issues. The International Labour Organization operates a "tripartite" system, under which unions and employers are each represented in addition to governments and help to frame the decisions reached. In the World Health Organization the representatives of the member-states are required to be medically qualified: and this too makes it better able to reflect the views of the medical profession throughout the world and not merely those of governments. There is no intrinsic reason why there should not be other specialized fora of a similar kind, in which the interest groups mainly concerned were represented, even in the main decision-making bodies, and so could feel that their voice had been heard in the decisions that were reached. Thus farmers' unions throughout the world could be afforded a special consultative status within the FAO; international scientific unions could be given a more formal and prominent role than today in discussions within UNESCO; the womens' organizations of the world could have a more recognized status in discussions of human rights within the Human Rights Commission; and so on.

In those ways the monopoly which is at present enjoyed by governments in the discussion of international issues might be gradually reduced. There would be increasing representation of the voice of many groups and individuals which have their own views on such questions, and an increasing opportunity provided for those views to be expressed. As the issues being discussed, and the interests to be protected, become increasingly global and non-national, global and non-national institutions would become available for discussing those issues and for protecting the interests of all those affected: the populations of the world generally and not only their governments.

Conclusions: A Global Polity

The developments we have traced in this book are mainly the result of one fundamental change in the environment within which political activity takes place: the decline of distance in the modern world.

The most obvious manifestation of this is the effect on personal mobility. Nobody is any longer any more than a few hours distant from any place in the world. This has a profound effect on economic relationships (creating a fast-integrating world economy), on social organization (causing migration and intermarriage on an unprecedented scale between states and continents); and on political contacts (leading for the first time to the creation of multi-national political movements and organizations).

But more significant still is the revolution in the communication of images and ideas. The capacity to transmit radio and television broadcasts or printed messages across the globe transforms the pictures of the world that are widely held. Frontiers, which were once dense and opaque barriers, are dissolved, becoming barely perceptible blips on the way to a much wider horizon. Those who live ten thousand miles away can now be reached as quickly, and can be seen and heard far more easily, than those who lived in the next village a century ago. The neighbourhood is no longer a few villages. It is a continent; even the world as a whole.

The area of interest and concern is widened as much as the area of knowledge. What happens in the next country is almost as well known as what happens in one's own. National boundaries no longer divide friend from foe, in-group from out-group, as for centuries before. Political ideas, loyalties, movements, classes and culture spread and spill across increasingly invisible national frontiers, becoming regional, even world-wide, in scope.

The change in political consciousness alters conceptions of political objectives: both the needs to be met and the means of meeting them. Political action at the national level is seen as increasingly irrelevant, except possibly as the means to international action. Tasks which were once seen as the responsibility of national governments to meet are now recognized as beyond their capabilities. National defence policies, national welfare policies, national environmental policies, national human rights policies, are no longer adequate; except possibly as component parts of international policies for the same purpose. Nor is sporadic cooperation among separate national units any longer a sufficient response to interdependence. Wider political structures altogether are required to meet the new needs. Political action of a different kind becomes necessary.

This applies above all to the task which has always been the most fundamental concern of political action: the creation of a more just society. Action within a national political or economic system, or even a regional one such as the European Community, cannot remedy the most important injustices of the modern world. Nothing which is done in any single state or region can bring about the kind of changes which are required. Whether a more left-wing or a more right-wing regime rules in the US, the Soviet Union or Britain, whether they privatize or nationalize, redistribute to the poor or grant tax benefits to the rich, will not in any way affect the most important distribution of power and wealth in contemporary society: that which exists between all, or almost all, who live in rich countries and all, or almost all, who live in poor ones. It is the maldistribution of benefits in the world as a whole, not within individual states, which is the concern of relevant political action today.

To create a more just international society only international action is significant. Only redistribution at the global level, through the establishment of a system of economic management comparable to that which operates within states, would be sufficient to remedy the types of inequality which are now most manifest. Only transnational political movements, bringing together those in all countries, rich or poor, concerned to bring about the type of changes required, are likely to bring about the adjustments in political and economic relations which would be necessary for that purpose. And only new international institutions, more representative than those which exist today, reflecting the views of groups and individuals as well as of governments, are likely to prove suitable instruments for bringing about such changes.

To some the call for changes of that order appear no doubt "Utopian", unrealistic and perhaps misguided. Yet only a century ago the demand for a fairer distribution of wealth and power, and for more fully representative political institutions, within states was equally seen by many as "Utopian", unrealistic or misguided. That did not prevent the emergence of political movements dedicated to bringing about such changes; nor stop them from in time achieving substantial progress towards those goals. With the speed of technical, political and social change in the modern world, it is not impossible that, in the global polity likewise, changes which appear impossibly remote today may, within the next century, appear equally attainable: perhaps even the condition of an acceptable political and economic order.

Politics has been globalized in part because inexorable technological change has had the effect that national endeavours are no longer adequate to achieve the goals which are everywhere demanded: the creation of a more peaceful, secure, environmentally acceptable life for the citizens of any state, free from the fear of military annihilation, environmental catastrophe or gross violations of their human rights. Because those tasks, even within states, today often require international rather than national action, political activity too must be international rather than national.

But political action is globalized also because, with the decline in distance, the goals themselves are transformed. A new political vision is created. Citizens are no longer content with the narrow and distorting aspirations created by parochial national political systems. They no longer accept that they share a common political destiny, similar political rights and political duties, only with those who happen to live under the same national flag as they do, but have no responsibilities for those who live under a different one; that poverty and hunger are a shame and an affront if they occur on their own side of the national frontier, but a matter of indifference when they occur on the other; that they must help to defend, with their taxes and with their lives if necessary, all those who sing the same national anthem as they do, but can turn their backs on those who sing a different one; that they have a responsibility to relieve the oppressed and succour the needy within their own national borders but that that responsibility stops abruptly as soon as they cross onto the other side. They know, and know increasingly, that they live on a small, and still shrinking, planet. They will not any longer obediently confine their responsibilities, and their concern, to conform with the lines that have been drawn at random across the atlas. On a planet so small they no longer have any choice but to be citizens of the world as a whole.

Index